# THE LAZY WITCHCRAFT GUIDE TO

# shadow work

# THE LAZY WITCHCRAFT GUIDE TO *shadow work*

75 PROMPTS, SPELLS, AND RITUALS FOR INNER TRANSFORMATION, HEALING, AND SELF-CARE

ANDREA SAMAYOA

FAIR WINDS

**Quarto.com**



First Published in 2026 by Fair Winds Press,
an imprint of The Quarto Group,
100 Cummings Center, Suite 265-D,
Beverly, MA 01915, USA.
T (978) 282-9590 F (978) 283-2742

EEA Representation, WTS Tax d.o.o.,
Žanova ulica 3, 4000 Kranj, Slovenia.
www.wts-tax.si



Fair Winds Press titles are also available at discount for retail, wholesale, promotional, and bulk purchase. For details, contact the Special Sales Manager by email at specialsales@quarto.com or by mail at The Quarto Group, Attn: Special Sales Manager 100 Cummings Center, Suite 265-D, Beverly, MA 01915, USA.

30 29 28 27 26     1 2 3 4 5

ISBN: 978-0-7603-9940-8

Digital edition published in 2026
eISBN: 978-0-7603-9941-5

Library of Congress Cataloging-in-Publication Data
available

Design and page layout: Samantha J. Bednarek, samanthabednarek.com
Illustrations: Kim Crago-Moon

Printed in Guangdong, China TT092025

I'd like to dedicate this book to
my brother, my boyfriend, and my
therapist for dealing with my bullshit.

# contents

# introduction

Hey there lazy witch! I'm BACKKKKKKK!

When I first started practicing witchcraft, I was at a major turning point in my life. I wanted a fresh start and to get rid of my shitty habits, fix my physical health, and do all the basic bitch things normal people talk about when they say cliché things like, "NEW YEAR, NEW ME!" But here's the thing: We're witches. We aren't normal.

See, I didn't just want a physical reset, I wanted a spiritual one as well. I needed my connection with my intuition and higher self to match the energy I was putting into the rest of my life. That's when I found shadow work (the process of uncovering and healing the hidden parts of yourself that feel rejected or "unfit" for the real world). It helped me face my traumas, confront the "bad" feelings we all try to hide, and make space for a deeper understanding of the universe, my soul, and my magic. Shadow work changed everything for me, and that's why I'm writing this book for you.

I want you to experience the same transformation I did without getting overwhelmed by the terminology, intimidated by heavy-ass questions, or scared of the whole process in general. Shadow work is messy but life-changing magic. And it doesn't need to feel like a lecture from your parent. I want it to feel like I'm guiding you as a friend.

In this book, we'll go through the shadow work process in three parts: preparation, navigation, and aftercare. Or, if it's easier to think about it this way: before, during, and after.

The first section, preparation, includes two chapters: one on cleansing and another on protection/grounding. I firmly believe that every witchy activity (or honestly anything that'll even slightly disturb your peace) should start with a cleanse and protect process. We need to wash away all the outside influences before we get into our shadow work so nothing fucks up our experience. Then, we lock that shit up with protection magic because we don't want any of that energy coming back unsolicited. We need to know that every discovery we make is from us and us alone.

The second section, navigation, is where we get into the good shit. We'll explore the history and origins of shadow work as well as why it's important to witches. Then, we'll set up and season our Shadow Work Journal, one of your most important tools in shadow work. It'll hold everything you work through, learn, and conquer on this journey. We'll use spells, correspondences, and intentional items to personalize your journal. Then we'll get into your shadow prompts, as well as spells and rituals to connect your witchcraft practice to your shadow work.

The last section of this book is dedicated to aftercare. Shadow work takes up time and energy, which can result in some pretty heavy emotional experiences. You absolutely have to take care of yourself afterward if you don't want to lose your mind. Think of shadow work like an intense therapy session. Are you going to leave the therapist's office and go straight to the club? Probably not. You'll most likely curl up on the couch with a nice warm blanket, a cup of tea, and cry a little. This section of the book is your warm blanket. We'll go over spells for healing, emotional support, courage, confidence, intuition, and spirituality, as well as other intentions that'll soothe your soul and relight whatever fire inside that started dwindling along the way.

As with my last book, *Lazy Witchcraft for Crazy Sh*tty Days*, all of the exercises, spells, and rituals in this book are designed to be as easy as possible so you don't burn yourself out while you're trying to heal and shit. I use the same spoon rating system as I did in the first book. One-spoon spells are the easiest and require the least amount of energy—think lighting a candle. Five-spoon spells are the "hardest," but that's usually just because they require, like, going outside, which you probably hate as much as I do. Intentions are provided in the ingredients lists, and there are also correspondence tables so you can swap things out so you don't have to waste a shit ton of money trying to track down one specific rare crystal or something.

So, grab a cup of tea, light a candle, wrap yourself in something warm, and let's fucking do this. Your soul is ready. You're ready. And I'm right here with you.

# PART 1

# PREPARATION: cleanse, protect, ground

Shadow work is the act of digging deep into your subconscious and discovering what's going on behind the scenes. Think of it like outpatient surgery. You open yourself up and dig around to find what's wrong. Then you take that part out to examine it, put it back in nice and neat, and close yourself back up. Imagine if you didn't clean the area before and after? Imagine if the hospital didn't sterilize the area before operating—and let anyone do the operation. That's what happens when you don't cleanse and protect yourself before or after your shadow work.

Without cleansing, the messages you find and discoveries you make when you're opening up old wounds will be confused and clouded with energy that isn't purely yours. When you aren't protected, you're allowing anyone or thing to enter your space while you're vulnerable. To avoid that, we'll start off this book with a couple of chapters on cleansing and protection so you can do your shadow work without the fear of outside influences.

But Andrea, you ask, what about this *grounding* stuff that you mentioned? Grounding is something that you should do in conjunction with your protection work. You don't need to do it for all of your magic, but it should be done for shadow work. Protection is about stopping outside forces from intruding on and draining your energy. Grounding is about making sure your *shadow self* doesn't drain that energy. Shadow work brings up the past and forces you to face things you don't like, which can send you into a spiral that drains your energy and makes you vulnerable to negative influences. Grounding stops the spiral. It stops your energy from being drained, helps you separate your thoughts from other people's thoughts of you, and strengthens the foundation of your protection work.

# 1

# cleanse + PURIFY

Do you ever wake up and feel *gross*? Like your energy is trying to work its way out of quicksand? You have a foggy mind and feel drained, overwhelmed. and emotional. Maybe your house feels "off" or your dreams are going wild for no apparent reason. Then, babe, you probably need to cleanse.

Cleansing is like hitting the reset button on your favorite video game—an energetic reset if you will. It doesn't fix your life and clear your debt, but it will clear out all that stagnant energy that makes you feel like you're drowning and losing your mind over every tiny task that comes your way. It helps you think more clearly and gives space for your shadow work to work more effectively. Think of it like a sink full of dirty dishes. Sure, you can clean just the dishes and be done, but if you leave the sink dirty did you even clean? Cleansing helps you release the bullshit instead of letting the bullshit sit there and accumulate fruit flies.

In this chapter, we'll go over cleansing correspondences, learn simple chants and techniques you can use for quick resets, and practice a few spells and rituals that are easy and effective for deeper cleansing. Let's get started.

# cleansing + purification CORRESPONDENCES

Here are your correspondences for cleansing and purification:

| Plants, herbs & flowers | Crystals & gemstones | Other shit |
|---|---|---|
| Angelica | Amethyst | **Color:** Blue, lavender, white |
| Basil | Black tourmaline | **Number:** 13 |
| Elderflower | Blue calcite | **Metal:** Gold, silver |
| Jasmine | Clear quartz | **Tarot:** Death, Temperance |
| Rosemary | Green fluorite | **Element:** Water, air |
| St. John's wort | Jade | **Zodiac**: Pisces, Libra |
| Yarrow | Smoky quartz | **Day:** Tuesday |

# low-spoon cleansing TECHNIQUES

There are a ton of different spells and rituals we can do to cleanse our space, and we'll get there later in this chapter. But sometimes a bitch is just too busy to be doing all that, ya know? (It's me, I'm that bitch who is too busy.) So here are some easy-as-fuck, low-spoon cleansing techniques you can do in between your deep cleanses. These are organized loosely from easiest to hardest (as hard as things get in lazy witchcraft), with a few options for each one.

## CLEANSING CHANTS

First up, cleansing chants. It literally does not get easier than this. You can use these on their own as a spoken word spell or with any of the other methods listed after this section.

- *I release what clings and clouds; I cleanse my soul from all that overcrowds.*
- *By will and might, ash and bone, I send this heaviness far from home.*
- *Cleanse the air, clear the heart, let fresh light in as we hit restart.*
- *Be gone old energy, I'm done with your shit. So it is done and no longer exists.*
- *Cleanse the static, end the noise. Clear out all but my inner voice.*
- *I call on wind, I call on flame; burn away what shouldn't remain.*
- *This is my space; this is my spell; all bad vibes can go to fucking hell.*
- *Darkness out, light in. Let the clearing now begin.*
- *Air and fire, do your part. Cleanse my mind and calm my heart.*
- *In this breath I let go of pain, cleanse my thoughts like summer rain.*
- *Clear my altar, clear my mind; all that's left is the divine.*
- *What was stuck is now released, I bless this space and claim my peace.*

## CLEANSING WITH TOOLS

Next up, we've got low-spoon cleansing methods that involve tools like smoke or sound. Remember, you can customize, combine, or adjust these in whatever way feels right.

### SOUND (1 TO 2 SPOONS)

When in doubt, make some fucking noise. Whether it's your voice or your favorite song, it'll clear energy out if you let it. Try:

**Clapping:** Clap as loud as you can while walking around your space, making sure to reach every corner of your home to scrape that old energy off the walls.

**Singing Bowls:** Originating in the Himalayas of Nepal and India, singing bowls are made to create vibrations that cleanse and align your energy.

**Bells and Chimes:** Placing a simple chime on your front porch is a perfect way to cleanse the energy of anything attempting to enter your space. Bells can easily be used before rituals to cleanse an altar and all its tools.

**Other:** Drumming, singing, chanting, and playing music are all fantastic ways to cleanse with minimal effort.

## LIGHT (1 TO 3 SPOONS)

When things feel dark, turn up the brightness. Literally. Light clears what shadows cling to. You can use:

**Sun and Moon Light:** Placing tools, crystals, or yourself in this natural light "burns" or "melts off" lingering energies.

**Candle Flames:** Moving around your space with a lit candle gets rid of energetic residues that we don't want.

**Visualization:** Visualizing golden lights washing over your body is the most common form of cleansing since it requires absolutely no ingredients to perform.

## SMOKE (2 TO 3 SPOONS)

Smoke is used to cleanse by many, many cultures for a large variety of reasons. As witches, we can use it to purify everything and anything, right down to our souls. You can:

**Light Incense:** Incense is a tried-and-true method. Choose a cleansing scent like cedar, chamomile, frankincense, rosemary, or sandalwood, and let the smoke do the work for you.

**Use Herbs:** Alternatively, you can combine herbs like juniper, angelica, yarrow, or mullein leaf in a mortar and pestle, grind them up, and burn them in a cauldron over a lit piece of charcoal.

## WATER (2 TO 4 SPOONS)

One of the ultimate cleansing methods is water. Super simple, right? Water is associated with healing, emotions, and purification, making the magic THAT MUCH EASIER to infuse. Here are few specific types to try:

**Moon Water:** Moon water is simply water that is charged for two to eight hours under the moon. Using new moon water for cleansing adds an extra intention boost since the new moon is ultimately associated with starting over, new beginnings, and getting rid of what no longer serves you.

**Florida Water:** Florida water was invented in the early 1800s as a cologne inspired by the Fountain of Youth. It is called Florida water specifically because the Fountain of Youth was said to be in Florida (it's also the Spanish word for flowery or floral). It became popular with Hispanic and African cultures because of its easy accessibility and safety. They could use the Florida water for rituals and spells without having to worry about the Christians finding out. It was primarily used for cleansing and blessing.

**Rainwater:** Rainwater is like magic falling from the fucking sky. It comes and washes away everything in its path. It literally gives the earth a shower and cleanses all the bullshit left by humanity.

**PRO TIP: Skip the smoke cleanse if you have asthma. It's not for us, baby.**

# one-herb cleansing SPELLS

Now that we've covered general cleansing methods, let's move on to one-herb, one-spoon spells. These mini spells are perfect for when the basics feel too basic but full spells and rituals seem like a lot. These spells are not meant to replace full cleansing rituals, just meant to get you by until your willpower returns.

## THE ELDERFLOWER NOTE

**ALL YOU NEED** for this spell is a pinch of elderflower, a piece of paper, and a pen.

On your paper, write: *I am cleansed, I am new. My space is clear, my mind has bloomed. With this paper and pen, my will is done. Elderflowers and intentions, all as one.*

Grab a pinch of your elderflower, close your eyes, and sprinkle it onto your paper. Fold the paper toward you once to bring that cleansing in. Fold the paper away from you once to send out all the shit that's not meant to stay.

Bury the paper in your backyard or in a trash can that is NOT inside your home.

## THE YARROW JAR

**FOR THIS SPELL,** you'll need a small jar with a cork, enough yarrow to fill about half the bottle, and a tiny paper with the word "purify" written on it.

Charge the paper with the word "purify" by holding it in your hands and repeating the word "purify" either in your head or out loud exactly thirteen times. (Don't worry, I count on my fingers too.)

Roll the tiny paper up, and place it inside the jar. The direction you roll the paper does not matter for this particular spell.

Add your yarrow to the jar. Bonus points if you place it in there by measuring it out in thirteen pinches instead of dumping it all at once.

Seal the jar with the cork, and place it on your altar. Whenever you need a small cleansing refresh, shake the jar.

# THE ROSEMARY SMOKE

**TO GET THIS SHIT DONE,** all you need is a fireproof plate, a lighter, and a rosemary bundle. If you do not have a rosemary bundle for whatever reason, you can use dried rosemary and a piece of charcoal to light the herb and produce smoke.

First, we're not hot boxing your home (that would be wild!), so open the fucking windows. Ignite that rosemary bundle with your lighter. Walk through every room in your house, and let the smoke fill each corner.

As you walk through, whisper any of the chants or affirmations you like from earlier in this chapter. You can repeat the same one, use all of them, or make up your own. And that's it! You're done. That's it. Super fucking easy.

# RITUALS FOR *deep cleansing*

Now that we've gone through the spells to hold you over, let's bring out the big guns and go over some full ritual methods that you'll use when your energy is high and your space is full of shit. Are they a tad harder than the stuff in the last section? Yes. Are they still easy as fuck? Also, yes.

## SUN & MOON HAND WASHES

**THIS SPELL WAS DESIGNED** to make your life easier in the long run by prepping a couple of magical hand washes in advance. Moon water is excellent for cleansing, but unfortunately it tends to cleanse EVERYTHING. Yes, the negative energy leaves the building but so does the positive. All the energy leaves. That's why we're pairing our moon wash with a sun wash. The sun water will restore all of the positive energy and good vibes the moon water might have accidentally kicked out.

There are so many situations in which these washes will come in handy: Use moon wash after waking up to release the energy of a nightmare and sun wash to bless you for the rest of your day. Use moon wash after a good cry or big emotional release to help clear the grief and sun wash to bring back peaceful and positive thinking. Use moon wash before casting a spell to release stale energy and then use sun wash to empower yourself. You get the idea. To use the washes, spray each hand twice, and then rub them together as if you're washing your hands for around one to two minutes. Give them a rinse, and you're good to go. (Sidenote: If the wash makes your hands sticky, you can use soap to get it off. The washes have already been incorporated into your aura and body, so it won't matter.)

**For the Moon Wash:**

8 ounces (235 ml) moon water

¼ cup (85 g) yarrow

¼ cup (18 g) St. John's wort

Clear quartz (chips or tumble)

**For the Sun Wash:**

8 ounces (235 ml) sun water

¼ cup (56 g) calendula

5 cinnamon sticks

Citrine (chips or tumble)

**For Both Washes:**

A pot and stove

Strainer

Two 4-ounce (120 ml) spray bottles

Essential or fragrance oils of your choice

1 ounce (28 ml) rubbing alcohol

Labels for each wash (optional)

The method for both washes will be the same so all you have to do is adjust the ingredients accordingly.

First, fill your pot with the water you're working with. Bring the water to a boil, and then turn it down to the lowest setting for a continuous rolling simmer.

Once your water is simmering, add the corresponding herbs, and recite the matching chant.

For the Moon Wash: *Moonlight come and wash me clean, take away all that's unseen. All energy I release, which allows me to step into quiet peace.*

For the Sun Wash: *Sunlight rays, I call it back. All positivity from each crack. I rise, I glow, I take my place. Bring back love and sacred grace.*

Let your washes simmer anywhere from fifteen to forty-five minutes.

The longer you leave it, the more potent your wash will be.

Once your wash is done simmering, turn your stove off, and let the wash cool all the way down to room temperature. Then strain out all the herbs, and transfer to your spray bottle, leaving room in the bottle for the crystals, oils, and rubbing alcohol. It's okay if there's leftover water. Pro tip: Funnels are great for people with shaky hands (like me).

Add in your corresponding crystal or crystal chips to the spray bottle. This will infuse the wash with the right energy and help mix everything together when you shake it. You can add essential or fragrance oils at this stage. Finish by filling the rest of the bottle with rubbing alcohol.

Repeat this process with the other hand wash. To keep organized, consider adding labels to each spray bottle.

# HOME CLEANSE & BLESS MINI RITUAL

**YOUR HOME IS SACRED.** It's where you eat, sleep, cry, learn, rest, love, and so much more. It keeps you safe from the physical elements of the world like hurricanes and pollen—fucking pollen!. It gives you a safe place to breathe. But just like a sponge, your home absorbs energy. Would you keep using the same sponge for years without dunking it in bleach every so often? Of course not. In this spell, we're giving our house an energetic bleach bath, then finishing it off with a blessing to add a little shine and create a bubble of positive energy around your most sacred space. I try to do this ritual once a month when I do my deep cleaning.

**You'll need:**

Your favorite music (see note)

Sandalwood or frankincense incense (and a holder, if needed)

3 white votive candles

3 pieces cleansing crystals (refer to table on page 14)

A pinch of basil for space cleansing and home blessing

A lighter or matches

Turn on your music and get ready to begin.

Start by setting up your mini ritual grid. Place your incense in the center of your work area and arrange the votive candles around it, leaving the same amount of space between each one. Add the crystals in between each candle.

Next, sprinkle a pinch of basil around the candles. I don't recommend sprinkling them on top of the candles because dried herbs do, in fact, catch fire.

Once everything is where the fuck it's supposed to be, it's time to light it up. Light your incense first and say:

*With this incense, I set the tone. Smoke and air fill my home.*

Next start lighting your candles ONE BY ONE. After the first one, say:

*Candle one, the spell has begun, cleanse this space and make us one.*

Close your eyes, and take one deep breath. Light the second candle and say:

*Candle two, this spell is glue, trap the bad energy and make it new.*

Close your eyes, and take two deep breaths. Light the last candle and say:

*Candle three, this spell is free, create the barrier, protect all of me.*

Close your eyes, and take three deep breaths. Imagine there's a giant bubble surrounding your home. Hold that image in your head for at least thirty seconds. (I know I know—I have ADHD too, so just try your hardest, okay?)

Let your candles burn as long as your incense is lit. Once the incense goes out, blow out your candles. You can reuse the candles and crystals for other spells—just let them sit in the moonlight overnight to cleanse the energy of this spell out of them.

**NOTE:** Use a playlist you listen to while physically cleaning your house on Sunday mornings.

# THE SHOWER CLEANSE

**VISUALIZATION IS ONE OF THE MOST ANCIENT FORMS** of manifestation and witchcraft in general, but when combined with ingredients and tools, the power is infinite. With this spell, you'll create a sachet to tie around your showerhead to bless the water flowing from it. There are also three different visualization techniques for shower cleansing so you don't get bored of the same old "imagine the water is gold" method.

**You'll need:**

A muslin sachet (see note)

Jasmine, for spiritual cleansing

Angelica, for emotional cleansing

St. John's wort, for cleansing and blessing

1 piece clear quartz, to purify

1 piece amethyst, to transmute negative energy into positive

Lavender or chamomile essential oil (optional)

First, create the sachet. In your bag, add in your herbs one by one, telling each of them exactly what they're doing there by using the intentions listed in the ingredients. Do the same for your crystals.

Once all your ingredients are in, pull the strings to close the bag, and tie it twice to seal the energy. You can add your optional essential oils to the outside of the bag by letting a few drops fall onto the fabric. This lets the shower steam release all that good-smelling energy as you wash up.

Tie your bag around the showerhead. Once you're ready, hop in, and start your shower as you normally would. You will begin visualization when you get to the shampoo stage of your shower. We'll use the shampoo to physically wash our hair clean and also to wash our souls. It's a "two birds, one stone" type of situation.

Use any one of the following methods for this part of the ritual. You'll notice each technique has an affirmation associated with it. If you can, try and chant it as you visualize. If you cannot, don't. Don't stress yourself out more than you need to.

**Method One: Black Smoke**

Imagine the negative energy leaving your body as a thick, dark fog that is expelled from your skin. If you have a window in your shower, visualize the fog leaving through the crack. If you don't, watch the fog disappear over the shower curtain and out the fucking door.

**Method Two: The Waterfall**

Imagine you're in a forest that's been enchanted by fairies and the goddess of the earth herself, Gaia. Picture the water coming from your showerhead as coming from a giant waterfall that you're standing right in front of. As the water hits your skin, see each droplet glowing white and fading away, purifying you from the outside in.

**Method Three: The Armor**
This method is easy. Visualize old habits, negative emotions, hatred, jealousy, etc. as a heavy suit of armor on your skin. As soon as the water touches you, this armor starts to melt off. Just make sure you also imagine it melting all the way down the damn drain.

Keep the sachet around your showerhead for up to three days. (Any more, and it'll start to mold and defeat the entire purpose of the spell. If you're like me and are 100 percent going to forget and leave it there, just take it the fuck down following your shower.) Then discard your used sachet outside of the home. I suggest doing this every two months; however, you can do the visualization techniques without the sachet as often as you need.

**NOTE:** In lieu of a sachet, you can also use little organza bags or even an empty tea bag.

# 2

# *protect +* GROUND

I will say this until I die: PROTECTION IS THE MOST IMPORTANT PART OF YOUR PRACTICE! NO MATTER WHAT. As a spiritual human, your mind, body, and energy are sacred AF and need to be protected. As a witch, you're like a fucking lighthouse. As a result, all the energy vampires and unseen bullshit out there will be that much more attracted to your spiritual energy. You must protect it.

Think of it like this: You're in a large group of people—let's say at a music concert. There are cameras. Imagine these cameras can only see two colors. Every nonwitchy, nonspiritual person shows up on the CCTV as a purple color. Every witchy, spiritual human shows up as a bright-ass yellow color. That is how we appear to energy vampires and other unseen dangers. When we do protection work, we're basically cloaking ourselves to look purple on that CCTV.

And grounding is your anchor. Protection keeps everything out, but grounding keeps *you* in. Protecting yourself without grounding clouds the protection spell's target (you) because you're everywhere but inside of your body.

This chapter includes all my easy, go-to protection and grounding spells, including correspondences, chants, mini spells, and full rituals.

# protection + grounding CORRESPONDENCES

Here are your correspondences for protection and grounding:

## PROTECTION CORRESPONDENCES

| Plants, herbs & flowers | Crystals & gemstones | Other shit |
|---|---|---|
| Agrimony | Angelite | **Color:** Black, blue, brown |
| Burdock root | Black onyx | **Number:** 3, 5, 9 |
| Chrysanthemum | Obsidian | **Metal:** Brass, copper |
| Cinnamon | Red jasper | **Tarot:** Strength |
| Mullein leaf | Smoky quartz | **Element:** Fire, earth |
| Rose | Tiger's eye | **Zodiac:** Cancer, Taurus |
| Rosemary | Tourmaline | **Day:** Saturday, Sunday |

## GROUNDING CORRESPONDENCES

| Plants, herbs & flowers | Crystals & gemstones | Other shit |
|---|---|---|
| Elderberry | Amethyst | **Color:** Brown, green |
| Juniper | Hematite | **Number:** 4, 8 |
| Lavender | Moss agate | **Metal:** Iron |
| Myrrh | Obsidian | **Tarot:** The Hermit |
| Patchouli | Smoky quartz | **Element:** Earth |
| Sandalwood | Tiger's eye | **Zodiac:** Taurus, Virgo |
| Vervain | Tourmaline | **Day:** Saturday |

# low-spoon protection TECHNIQUES

Since protection is pretty much this important to all witches, we've come up with an endless number of ways to protect ourselves. Just like our last chapter, I'm going to start with some super-easy, low-spoon techniques you can do to protect yourself on the fly. These are organized more or less from easiest to "hardest," with a few options for each one.

## PROTECTION CHANTS

The following chants and affirmations can be used solo or in conjunction with any of the protection methods listed later in this section.

- *From head to toe, I cast this shield. With sacred force, a minefield.*
- *By earth and fire and wind and sea, all bad intent will stay away from me.*
- *I stand in power, running deep. No ill or curse shall be able to touch me.*
- *No energy may stay that is not mine; no enemies can enter my psychic mind.*
- *Stars above and roots below, I am protected wherever I go.*
- *I am safe, I am secure. My ward walks with me and keeps my pure.*
- *Not today, not ever. My energy is locked. That bullshit can miss me, it is blocked.*
- *Fuck your will, and fuck your might. My protections are powerful, and they definitely bite.*
- *I walk in strength; I walk in fire. No curse or hex can cut this wire.*
- *My space is mine, my soul is free. No dark my dwell near me.*
- *Wards are set, the wall is thick. Evil energy will never stick.*
- *The entry is closed, the seal is tight. Only love and healing may cross this line.*

## PROTECTING WITH TOOLS

Now let's go over easy protection and grounding methods that don't require a full spell. These work with the same elements we worked with in the cleansing chapter with adjusted intentions to work for defense and stability.

### SOUND (1 TO 2 SPOONS)

Sound isn't just for cleansing; it can also build a strong wall to keep the bullshit out. The right vibration can cut through and hold your spiritual space like a strong shield. Try:

**Clapping:** Simply clapping your hands breaks up negative energy and seals the space.

**Bells:** Ringing bells around your doors and windows wards off bad vibes.

**Chimes:** Hanging chimes repels negative energy as it comes into your home, stopping it in its tracks.

**Other Ways:** Playing heavy music (metal, EDM), drumming to push out energy, and using tuning forks creates a sacred shield around your body before you leave your house.

### LIGHT (1 TO 3 SPOONS)

Light doesn't just reveal. It defends. Use it to push out darkness and reinforce your energetic boundaries.

**Visualization:** Visualize a thick, black wall or bubble around yourself when you need a quick protective shield.

**Lanterns or Flashlights:** Traditionally, lanterns were lit at doorways, crossroads, or windows to ward off spirits and protect travelers.

### SMOKE (2 TO 3 SPOONS)

Across many cultures, smoke is seen as a carrier. Think of it like a carrier pigeon. Carrier pigeons are ancient breeds known to send messages using the earth's magnetic field to navigate. When you burn herbs, the smoke's spiritual carrier pigeon is activated. It carries the herbs' intentions into the universe, spreading them far and wide.

Burn herbs like rosemary, cedar, mugwort, or mullein leaf to create a protective boundary around your space. Bay leaves are perfect for this since they're naturally protective, and you can draw warding sigils (see page 33) on them to get an extra power boost.

Alternatively, burning scented candles with a candle heating lamp eliminates the smoke but still uses the element of air to carry the protective scents around your home. Bonus points if the candles are scented with cinnamon or rosemary for extra protection correspondences.

### WATER (2 TO 4 SPOONS)

In ancient Egypt, it was believed that you could charge water with words, incense, or intention to shield against evil. The Greeks and Romans believed drinking from springs and wells could ward off "spirits of illness." The Christians have their holy water, which they use to ward off demons during exorcisms. We, too, have our own witchy ways of using water to protect ourselves.

**Salt:** Adding salt to your bath and soaking in it for five to ten minutes can help build or strengthen energetic shields. Alternatively, you can take a shot of salted water to protect yourself internally. It's kinda gross, but if you're into it, extra points.

**Moon Water:** Full moon or waning moon water uses the protective energies from either moon phase to give you a powerful bowl of "stay the fuck away from me" energy.

**Oils:** Oils count as water as well. Oils infused with any protective herb or crystal can be carried with you as an emergency protection ward when placed on your pressure points (wrist, temples, feet, palms, third eye, etc.).

# one-herb protection SPELLS

Now that we have the basics down, let's move on to some slightly more focused mini spells that are still easy but give an extra boost of protection magic. Here are some powerful one-herb spells to keep your energy guarded as fuck.

## THE CINNAMON BREW

**TO CAST THIS SPELL,** you'll need three cinnamon sticks, a mug of hot water, and a spoon.

Place your cinnamon sticks in the mug of hot water and let them soak for three to four minutes. When they're done, remove the sticks and use your spoon to stir the water clockwise to bring in protection.

While you drink the tea, set the cinnamon ward by closing your eyes and visualizing a bubble of protection around you. You're done!

## THE BURDOCK SALT

**FOR THIS MINI RITUAL,** you'll need a bit of burdock root, a small jar or container, and salt (any kind of salt).

Add the burdock root to the jar, telling the herb what it's there for while you do:

*Burdock root, protect me from harm, stop all incoming evil, and keep me grounded.*

Next, fill the jar with salt, leaving a little bit of space at the top of the jar so you can shake it and get it all mixed in well. While you add the salt, tell it what it's doing. Say something like:

*Listen, salt, I know you know why you're here. Bind the burdock and strengthen its power.*

Shake the jar as hard as you can. If people are in your immediate vicinity, they should be looking at you like you're fucking insane.

Use the salt in spell jars, around candles, on your windowsills, on your altar, or to charge your tools. Use it for whatever the fuck you want, whenever the fuck you want.

## THE MULLEIN LEAF STICK

**FOR THIS SPELL,** you'll need some sort of natural paper (like rice paper, which burns slowly) and a little bit of mullein leaf. The paper should be around 3 to 4 inches (7 to 10 cm) long and 2 to 3 inches wide.

Lay the paper in front of you and sprinkle the mullein leaf down the middle of the paper in a vertical line. As you sprinkle the herb, choose one of the protection chants from earlier in this chapter (see page 29) and recite it.

Roll the paper into a cone and twist both ends. Light one end and walk around your home, letting the smoke fill each corner. The mullein leaf will drive all the evil bullshit away and keep it out.

Let the paper burn out on its own, and save it to reuse whenever you want.

## THE ROSEMARY FLAME

**FOR THIS SPELL,** you will need a black candle (of any kind) and dried rosemary.

If you're using a **tealight**, **votive**, or **jar candle**, sprinkle the rosemary directly on the wax, making sure it doesn't go near the wick. If you're using a **chime**, **taper**, or **pillar candle**, hold the candle in your hands for a few seconds to slightly heat it up, then roll the rosemary onto the candle. Remember, the candles don't need to be fully covered with rosemary—just enough to count. Once the rosemary is on your candle, whisper this chant:

*Wax and herb, fire, and earth. Protect this space and home and hearth. Give me power to keep these wards, hard as rock and sharp as sword.*

You can either light the candle now and let it burn all the way down or light it for two to three minutes at a time every day until the candle is gone. It really just depends on your mood.

# RITUALS FOR *serious protection*

Now we've made it to the big guns. I'm not saying big as in complicated; I'm saying big as in powerful. In this section, we'll cover full rituals to seriously protect and ground your energy and space.

## PROTECTION OIL BLEND

**OIL BLENDS ARE SUPER EASY** to make and pack a POTENT punch. I made the process for this oil especially easy—you don't even need a fucking strainer.

**You'll need:**

1 ounce (28 ml) dropper bottle

Incense, for cleansing

Smoky quartz chips, for negativity absorption and grounding

Tiger's eye chips, for strength and confidence

Angelica, for divine protection and hex breaking

Agrimony, for banishing negative energy

2 tablespoons (30 ml) castor oil (or any carrier oil, see page 123)

Start by cleansing your bottle with any kind of incense. We want to make sure the bottle is pure as fuck and nothing external will interfere.

Add everything in, one by one, minus the oil. Remember to set your goddamn motherfucking intentions, bitch. How are you setting intentions this time? My witch, it's a one-spoon spell. Just read the intentions I provided in the ingredients list. You can repeat the intention until you move on to the next ingredient, or hold it in your hands, whisper it, and move on.

Once all the ingredients are in, add your carrier oil, secure the lid, and you're done. Use it however the fuck you want, whenever the fuck you want. I suggest using it on pressure points, so think behind the ears, third eye, wrists, soles of feet, etc. You can also use it to make a "seal" around windows and door thresholds or even to dress candles.

# PROTECTION SIMMER POT

**THIS SIMMER POT RITUAL BLEND** is ideal for witches who live in their kitchen and/or witches who are lazy as fuck. (If you're reading this book, maybe you're both.) We will prep a full jar of simmer pot goodness, so when you're feeling like you need some extra protections, you can dump the complete blend into your pot of water and let it simmer away, doing the magic for you. That said, since we want this to be easy as fuck for our future selves, we have to infuse the intention during this phase.

**You'll need:**
An edible marker or nontoxic, water-based marker

5 unbroken bay leaves (or, like, mostly unbroken)

A large bowl

1 cup (13 g) dried rosemary, for spiritual protection

1 cup (60 g) galangal root, for psychic protection

1 cup (128 g) dried roses, for emotional protection

1 cup (112 g) dried chrysanthemum flowers, to ward off evil

5 small containers (see note)

50 drops frankincense oil (optional)

10 cinnamon sticks, to power boost the spell

With your edible marker, start adding your sigils to the bay leaves. (If you don't remember how to make a sigil, refer to page 33.) On the first bay leaf, draw a sigil for protection. On the second, draw a sigil for warding. On the third, draw a sigil for banishing. On the fourth, draw a sigil for defense. On the last bay leaf, draw a sigil for yourself, using your name.

Once all the bay leaves are prepared, crush each one into the bowl with your hands, one at a time. While you crush each leaf, keep the word the sigil represents in your head. This'll strengthen that intention.

Next, slowly sprinkle a cup of rosemary into the bowl. Say: *Rosemary rise, spirit protection hold. Keep me safe, strong, and bold.*

Next add the galangal root. Say: *Root of fire, shield my mind. Maintain my clarity and piece of mind.*

Next, add your roses and say: *Rose and thorn, guard my heart. Preserve the structure of each part.*

Last, add your chrysanthemum. Say: *Chrysanthemum guard, spirits go. Keep my spirit's very bright glow.*

Use your hands to mix up all the herbs in the bowl. Really get all up in there. You want your magic to flow from your hands into the herbs.

Portion the mix out into five parts and place them into your containers. If you're adding the frankincense oil, do that now. Use ten drops per batch, right on top.

Hold your cinnamon sticks in your hands. Say: *Fire sticks, bring the heat. Make this ward powerful indeed. One by one I add them in, their spice and heat seal the magic within.*

Add two sticks to each batch and close the container. Store your batches in a cool, dark place until you're ready to use them.

To use the blend, simply add ½ to 1 cup of your herb blend to a pot of boiling water. Bring the water down to a simmer, and let it sit for three to four hours. When you're done, you can discard the contents like you normally would, or you can save the water and make it into a protection spray.

**NOTE: Your small containers can be anything from zip-top sandwich bags to glass jars with cork tops to mason jars. It quite literally does not matter; it just needs to be able to fit the spell prep mix.**

# THE GROUNDING SIGIL

**I'VE ALWAYS SAID** that sigils are just personal runes. It's a symbol you create using one or multiple words and intentions. You can make sigils for any kind of spell; this one is for grounding. I will show you (in the easiest terms possible) how to create a sigil and activate it.

**You'll need:**
A nontoxic marker

A piece of paper

Tweezers or tongs

Fireproof plate

A lighter

First, spell out your word or phrase (I usually always do it in caps) on a piece of paper. I've made each letter a different color so you can follow along.

Now, you'll break down each letter into the basic lines that make it up. These don't have to be perfect, so just relax and go with the flow.

Now, combine those lines to form a sigil. You can add extra flair with dots, squiggles, or other symbols.

And that's it. If you're still feeling a little uncomfy about it, you're more than welcome to copy or trace mine. Sidenote: If you make your own sigil, put a copy in your Shadow Work Journal so you don't forget what it looks like and can reuse it whenever. Your book of shadows is like your personal spell book. Its where you hold all spells, research, information, and notes. Not to be confused with the Shadow Work Journal we'll be setting up in the next part of this book.

Now that your sigil is done, it's time to activate it. There are many ways to do this, but the most common way is to burn it. Grab your tweezers, hold the paper over your fireproof plate, and light it. Use the ash to make black salt or blow it away in the wind, and you're done. Your sigil is activated. Redraw the sigil anywhere, at any time, on anything to infuse it with grounding power.

# CRYSTAL GRID FOR GROUNDING

**FIRST OFF, GROUNDING IS A LIFE SAVER.** Between my ADHD, my autism, and my undiagnosed chronic illness, my mind goes blank and wonders off A LOT. The only thing that brings me back to the moment and quiets the million tasks running through my brain at all times is grounding. When we make a crystal grid, we're using corresponding gems to create a focused energy structure. Think of it like a computer: The individual crystals are the internal bits that make up the computer, each with a specific task. The grid itself is the computer and the energy that comes off of it is like connecting to the Internet. We don't see the magic, but it's there. In this spell, we will create a grounding powerhouse that can be kept anywhere in your home and also doubles as some pretty beautiful home décor.

**You'll need:**

Sand or salt (enough to cover the surface of the plate)

A circular plate

1 piece clear quartz

6 pieces tiger's eye

4 pieces moss agate

6 pieces black tourmaline

Pour the sand or salt all over the plate, and spread it out into a thin, even layer. This will help the crystal stay in place when you need to move it around.

Place the clear quartz in the center of the plate. The quartz is the powerhouse of the cell. It will keep the energy charged and focused.

Next, hold your tiger's eye pieces in your hand. Close your eyes and imagine a gold light glowing around your hands and transferring to the tiger's eye. This is infusing strength, courage, clarity, and protection. Place them on the plate according to the illustration at right.

Now hold your moss agate pieces in your hand and close your eyes. Imagine a dark forest-green color glowing from your hands and transferring into the crystals. This is infusing earth energy, emotional balance, and guidance. Place them on the plate according to the illustration.

Last, hold your black tourmaline in your hands and close your eyes one last time. Imagine a copper-colored glowing light radiating from your hands and seeping inside of each crystal. This is infusing grounding energy, absorbing negativity, and promoting growth. Place them on your plate according to the illustration.

Place your grid in the center of the home. (Yes, the floor is totally fine if you don't have pets. If you do, get as close as you can to the floor.) Leave it there for twenty-four hours. Once the time is up, place the grid on your altar and leave it up for as long as your heart desires.

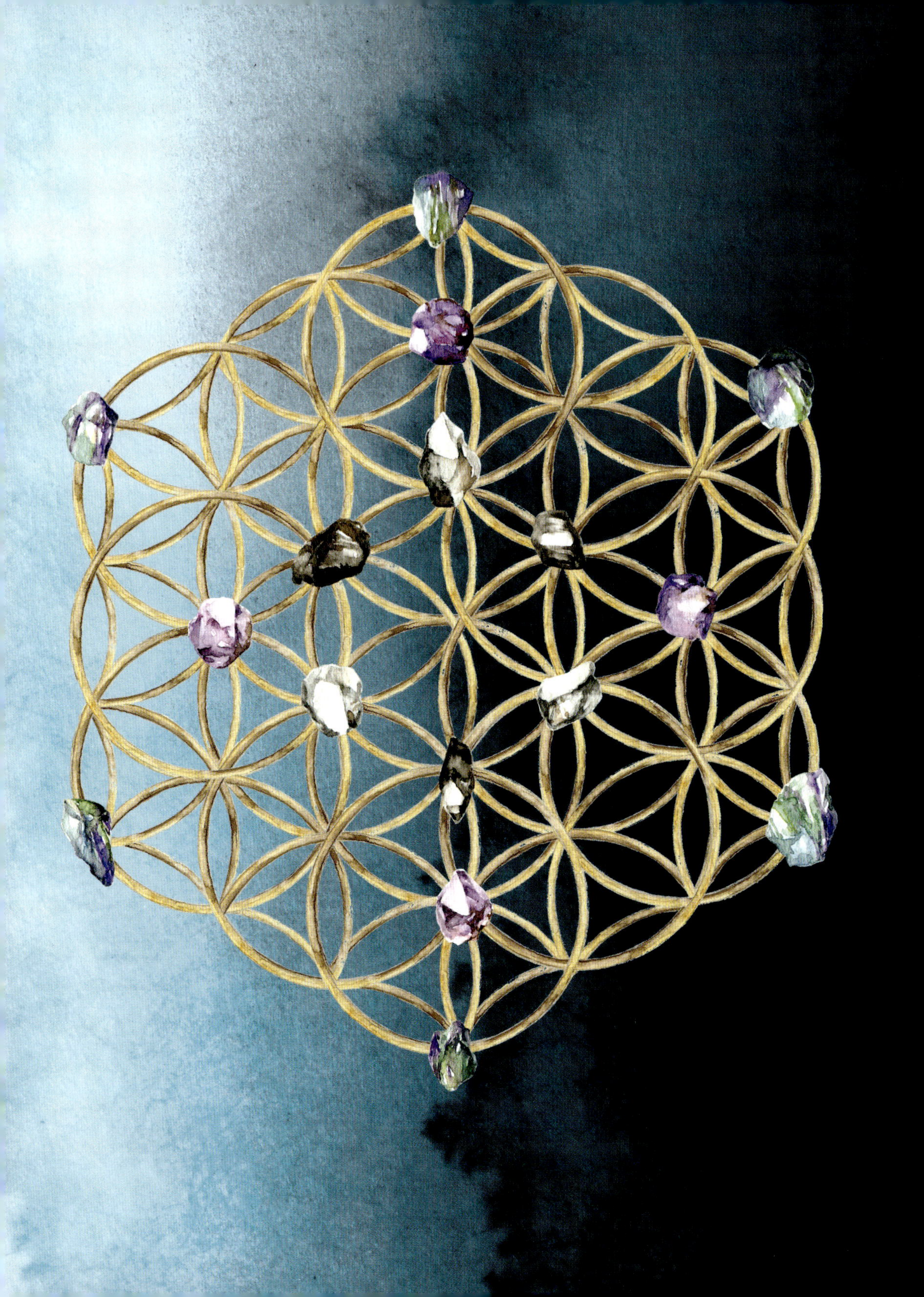

# CLEANSE & PROTECT DETOX SHOTS

**OUR FINAL SPELL FROM PART ONE** covers both cleansing AND protection for a neat little two-for-one treat. This spell invites you to detox the fuck out of your soul with a couple of cleansing and protective herbal shots. But wait, no, there's no alcohol. Unless you're over the legal drinking age—then I suggest adding some tequila to the protection brew and some gin to the cleansing one because who am I to tell a grown adult what to do, ya know?

You'll take these shots twice a day, morning and night, for three consecutive days. The shots will not last longer than that, so make sure you follow these instructions or you will just waste them. Alternatively, you can prep the herbs in batches and brew when needed. Most of this spell is totally up to you and what works for your specific lifestyle. Always double-check how herbs affect allergies, medications, pregnancy, or health conditions before using them.

**You'll need:**

2 empty tea bags or ball strainers

1 tablespoon (5 g) chamomile, for emotional cleansing

1 teaspoon (7 g) yarrow, for spiritual purification

1 teaspoon (1 g) basil, for overall cleansing

1 tablespoon (6 g) black tea, for protection

½ teaspoon cinnamon, for warding

½ teaspoon rosemary, for grounding

2 mugs

6 ounces (175 ml) hot water

Two (2 ounce or 60 ml) bottles or jars with lids

½ ounce (14 ml) gin (optional)

½ ounce (14 ml) tequila (optional)

The method for this spell is super straightforward. First, prepare your tea bags or strainers. In the first bag or strainer, combine the chamomile, yarrow, and basil. This bag is for cleansing. In the second bag, combine the black tea, cinnamon, and rosemary. This bag is for protection.

Fill two mugs each with 3 ounces (90 ml) of hot water. Add the cleansing bag you just made to one of them. Wave your hands over the mug and say: *Cleanse my heart, soul, mind, spirit, and body.*

Place your protection bag in the other mug, wave your hands over it, and say: *Protect my heart, soul, mind, spirit, and body.*

Let your cleansing tea brew for thirteen minutes and your protection brew for six minutes. Set timers to make sure you don't let anything over-steep.

Once the teas are done steeping, remove the bags and discard them in the trash. Or save them, dry them out, and use them as incense if you're feeling extra.

Let the teas cool completely. Then pour them equally into two separate 2-ounce (60 ml) jars. If you choose to add the alcohol to your shots, you can do this now. In the morning, take the first shot of your cleansing potion. At night, take a shot of your protection potion. Think of it like antibiotics; if you miss a dose, you'll probably have to start over. Store the remainder of the shots in the fridge.

For the next two days, take each shot around the same time, morning and night. On the last day, say: *Three days have passed, my spell is sealed. What was hidden is now healed. The work is done, the path is clear. I walk with power, I hold no fear.*

Once your detox is done, you can clean the jars and reuse them for next time. I highly recommend doing this before any shadow work session to open your mind a little more than it already is and protect whatever peace you have.

# PART 2

# DO YOUR FUCKING shadow work

Before we begin this section, I'd just like to state that shadow work is an intense process. I'm not trying to scare you because it is one of the most effective ways to become self-aware; however, if you're already struggling with your mental health, I highly suggest speaking with your therapist to see if they could work though some of the more intense ideas and exercises in this section with you. I've done shadow work on my own, with my therapist, and with my partner. All of these approaches were equally effective, so don't feel bad if you need to bring a buddy.

There are a lot of misconceptions about shadow work, so let's bust some of those right now:

1. Shadow work is not dangerous or evil. Listen, I too thought the same thing when I first heard about shadow work simply because of the fucking name.
2. You don't need to relive trauma to heal it. Meaning, you don't need to reenact the entire experience; you just need to remember the emotions that resulted from said trauma. If you're easily triggered by an intense experience from your past or have not processed a specific trauma enough, this is where you should bring in a second person to be a witness.
3. Shadow work doesn't have to be an overwhelming or constant process. You don't need to do it every day, every week, or even every month. Shadow work is meant to be taken at your own pace, on your own time. You're not failing if you only do a little bit each month, I promise.
4. Shadow work is not just for witches. It's a universal tool.

And here's the biggest misconception of all: Shadow work should NEVER be confused with toxic positivity. In fact, they're opposites: Toxic positivity slows down your progress by pushing all the shit down and never doing anything about it, while shadow work teaches us how to navigate and heal from the past traumas that trigger these feelings. When we do shadow work, we're honoring the light and the darkness. It's an act of acceptance rather than an act of denial.

Now that we've got that out of the way, let's begin.

# 3

# YOUR shadow work JOURNAL

This chapter is your introduction to shadow work and the most important tool you'll use on your journey to self-acceptance: your journal. You can't face what you don't fucking understand, so we'll start by breaking down what shadow work actually is, from its history and meanings to how your shadow self is connected to your life and witchcraft. I'll show you how to set up a shadow work altar and how to prepare, enchant, and activate your journal. Finally, we'll discuss how to use the journal, and I'll provide some prompts to get you started. Ready to face your shit? Let's go.

# A DEEP DIVE INTO shadow work

What we know today as shadow work was first invented by Carl Jung, a Swiss psychiatrist and psychotherapist from the nineteenth century. While he originally studied to be a psychologist and was BFFs with Freud, he went in a different direction with his theories, attempting to link mysticism, spirituality, and the unconscious with the psyche. Jung had the vision that there were three main parts to your psyche (there's actually, like, nine of them, but this is lazy witchcraft, not a psychology course, so let's stick to three):

- **The conscious:** This is the part we show the world. Our thoughts, our intentions. This is what we identify with the most and what helps us with logical decision-making (even if you're slightly unhinged).
- **The personal unconscious:** This is what we've subconsciously hidden. Memories we think we forgot, unhealed trauma—everything we're putting in the back of our mind to forget about goes here. This is also where we hide our "bad" traits, such as anger, fear, judgment, jealousy.
- **The collective unconscious:** This is what we, as a society, unconsciously have learned to be true. This is where our societal archetypes/roles live (you know: the maiden, the mother, the crone, etc.). This is where our brain keeps myths, social cues, instincts, and societal influences.

Jung's theory was that we, as humans, naturally hide the parts of ourselves that society has told us are "bad." This is your shadow self: the person, emotions, and experiences you hide from the world; your anger with no release; your jealousy; your frustration; your unhealed trauma; etc. To free ourselves from these feelings and experiences, we must explore them. Basically, we need to embrace what makes us uncomfortable before we can be fully free. This process of exploration is called shadow work.

When we do shadow work, we're going through our personal unconscious and collective unconscious because those are, quite literally, the core of what make up our shadow traits. Of course, these vary highly by your personality, the way you grew up, and the things you've done. Shadow work is both a very personal thing and a very shared experience. Super weird, right?

## WHY SHADOW WORK MATTERS TO WITCHES

Why does all this matter to witches? Your witchcraft comes from your personal energy, which is ruled by your emotions and feelings. Shadow work helps us explore and integrate our darker emotions and feelings—the parts of us that are unhealed, unresolved, and unworthy (in our eyes). It improves our self-awareness by identifying and exploring issues and causes of the issue that are creating blockages to our energy. It helps us be more confident in our own skin by understanding who TF we are and lets us use our shadow selves in harmony with other supposedly "friendlier" traits. It also helps build our connections with our intuition, our guides, and our relationships in general.

Now, you might be thinking, my life's not so bad—do I really need this? BESTIE, YES. Everyone has experienced shit, and that shit can be traumatizing. Even if you think you're "over it," shit can still affect you without you even knowing it. Imagine you're chillin' on the couch and someone shows up at your house and forces you to run a marathon with no shoes and no stretching. You really think that's not going to affect you after it's over? It absolutely is. Trauma works the same way: You can't go from a very emotional experience to a normal, functioning day without some care and processing. You can try to put it off, and you can try to bury it, but it's going to show up eventually. And that's when you need to do your fucking shadow work.

## HOW DO I KNOW I NEED SHADOW WORK?

Well, everyone does. But here are some specific signs you need shadow work in your life:

- **Reoccurring Negative Patterns:** Do you always end up crying over the same thing? Are you always angry? Are you always sad? Are you a mix of these? Do you keep exhibiting negative habits and traits that are harmful to yourself and others?
- **Feeling Stuck:** Does it feel like no matter what you do, you can't move on to the next step in life? Do you procrastinate a lot? Do you feel helpless when attempting to change or improve your life? Do you feel like you want to grow but are just so fucking unmotivated?
- **Easily Triggered:** Do you overreact a lot and then come back later and say, "Wow, actually that was wild of me"? Do you get set off by the tiniest of inconveniences? Are there specific people, places, things, and experiences that just send you right over the edge?

- **Avoidance:** Are you avoiding certain emotions or memories? Do you avoid specific scenarios that happen often? Do you avoid tasks or conversations even when you know you need to address that shit?
- **Feeling Disconnected:** Do you feel like your spells aren't working? Do you feel like you can't connect to the universe when setting intentions? Do you second-guess your intuition and find out later that you were right the first time? Are you just going through the motions but not feeling the same relationship you used to have with your magic?

These signs are manifestations of our shadow emotions or shadow traits. And, honestly, the more shadow work you do, the more they will show up. Shadow work is about getting answers as to why we are the way we are, but to do that you've got to wade through the thick, unpleasant mud that is your unhealed trauma. You can't go around it; you have to go through it. Think of it like a small puddle of quicksand. The quicksand is your trauma. Its job is to pull you down until you sink. Shadow work is like the rope you'll use to pull yourself out, and as you're doing that, your shadow traits are going to sound off. These emotions aren't bad; they're not meant to scold you or get you in trouble. They simply show you which parts of yourself have been neglected.

Other shadow emotions and traits that may appear while you're working through unprocessed trauma can include:

- Anger
- Defensiveness
- Fear
- Guilt
- Insecurity
- Jealousy
- Loneliness
- Need for control
- Overcompensation
- Perfectionism
- Projection
- Resentment
- Sadness
- Self-sabotage
- Shame

Now, does doing a couple rounds of shadow work mean you'll be completely healed and never experience these bad feelings again? Absolutely not. No one is fucking sunshine and roses 24/7—that would be absolutely insane. Shadow work helps you embrace all of your emotions—the bad shit and the good shit. Suppressing hard feelings is what you're doing right now, and the goal is to get to a place where those emotions live rent-free in your head without you feeling like you need to hide them. We're not trying to hold onto these emotions because we think they're good for us, but we do need to bring them to the front and work though them so we can ultimately use them for good. Your journal will be the main tool you use to do this. Before we get to that, though, we need to do a little more prep work to set the tone and make sure we have a safe space for our journey. In other words, we need to make a fucking altar.

# PREPARING YOUR shadow work altar

We all know vibes are the main focus in witchcraft, generally speaking. If the vibes are off, your spell work feels off, and, ultimately, it's not going to work as well as it could. To assist us with said vibes, we need to create a sacred space where you and your shadow self can be comfortable enough to exchange feelings. This is your shadow work altar.

Your altar is your home base. You can use it as your main journaling spot or just somewhere to hold and charge your journal. It can be permanent, temporary, super organized, a whole fucking mess, or anything in between. You know how people always say, "My ancestors tell me how much salt to add" when cooking recipes? That's exactly what this is. Trust yourself, trust your intuition, and do what feels right to you alone.

A shadow work altar can be made up of lots of different items, and I've included some ideas below to get you started. To be clear, you don't need everything I list here. Choose whatever works for you and your space. As you grow, write, learn, and explore, you can swap out crystals and items that better match exactly what you're trying to accomplish with your shadow work. Remember, there is absolutely no need to spend hundreds of dollars creating this. Try using items you already have or are easily found around your house or backyard or at your local bargain discount store.

## CRYSTALS

There are a few specific types of crystal that are especially beneficial for shadow work:

- Pink crystals, like rose quartz, help ease the emotions coming to the surface.
- Blue crystals, like blue calcite, help you connect to your higher beings, making it easier to navigate shadow work prompts and rituals.
- Black crystals, like obsidian, help protect you from destructive inner dialogue and self-loathing thoughts. We want to explore and discover but *safely.*
- White and clear stones, like selenite or clear quartz, help with healing and making the weight of all this bullshit a little lighter.

## HERBS

Making a couple shadow work herb blends ahead of time will make your life so much easier in the long run. I like to keep two blends on hand, so I'll show you those. However, please note that if you only have one herb from each blend, it's more than enough. Just use the same technique I describe below to infuse your intention into the herb. Please note that these blends are not for consumption.

# SHADOW WORK HERB BLENDS

**Herb Blend for Healing and Emotions**
Choose three: lavender, rose petals, yarrow, basil, lemon balm, sea salt, angelica, chamomile, sandalwood

**Herb Blend for Protecting Your Spiritual Self**
Choose three: black salt, rosemary, mugwort, juniper, galangal, frankincense, myrrh, agrimony, St. John's wort

To create these blends, literally just mix all of the herbs you've chosen for each blend in separate jars, and keep them on your altar. You don't need to set intentions while making the blends, because the intent will be more potent if you infuse it right before using it. To infuse your energy, simply take a bit in the palm of your left hand, place your right hand on top, and say: *I infuse this blend with magic and light, my intent is what is right. Let these herbs ________ me, carrying my spirit in gentle flight. As it is said, as it shall be.*

Fill in the empty space with the word "protect" or "heal," depending on the blend.

Uses for the herb blends include making protective and healing circles before journaling, lighting them as loose incense (please research which herbs are and aren't safe to burn before doing that), dressing candles, sticking them in spell jars, using them in offering bowls, and so many other things.

## TAROT CARDS

Tarot cards are a great addition to a shadow work altar. Personally, I like to use the Moon, the Star, and the Sun in my practice because, when combined, they basically break down the cycle of each shadow work session.

The Moon helps us navigate darkness and reveals the truth behind our shadow work. This is what the **start** of our shadow work sessions need.

The Star brings balance, clarity, and spiritual guidance to assist you in figuring out what the fuck is actually going on with your soul without overwhelming it. This is what helps us **during** our shadow work sessions.

The Sun gives a sense of accomplishment and success while also healing and shifting your mindset back to optimism rather than the doom and gloom that sometimes comes from these sessions. This is how we **close** our session without just abruptly saying, "Aiiight, that was fun. I'm out." Ya know?

## OFFERINGS

I'm very fond of placing offerings on my altar. It's an easy way to ask the universe for assistance or thank it for assisting you throughout this journey. (Because, honestly, imagine if you were doing this with no witchcraft? That shit would suck.)

I like to keep a bowl or chalice in the center of my altar to make giving offerings much easier. Your offerings don't need to be things on my list; you can offer things that correspond with your deity, your higher power, the earth, the universe, etc. This list is more of a generic "all higher powers" offerings.

When you place your offering in your vessel of choice, remember to SET YOUR MF-ING INTENTIONS, BITCH. How do I do that lazy witchcraft style? I repeat "thank you" a total of eleven times. One hundred and eleven is the angel number associated with alignment, manifestation, and clarity and often acts as a "gratitude amplifier" because of its intention-boosting powers. And since I know for a fact none of us is going to sit here and repeat the words "thank you" one hundred and eleven times, we'll stick with eleven.

Things you can use as offerings include rice, alcoholic drinks (the earth is fond of red wine), fruits, jewelry, teas, waters, handcrafted art—anything you think the guides would like. Note that you'll need to discard any food or drinks you use as offerings before they begin to mold. An exception would be straight liquor because it usually evaporates on its own. Please don't let your house get filled with ants because you're trying to be magical.

## OTHER ITEMS

Other items you can place on your shadow work altar include:

- **Mirrors** are perfect for shadow work altars because they signify self-reflection in the most literal way.
- **Magazine or book cutouts** of your favorite poems or phrases.
- **Statues or figurines** of the earth, Gaia, or celestial beings are more literal ways to focus your intentions.
- **White candles** for healing or **black candles** for protection.
- **Bells, drums,** or **singing bowls** are great at aligning your intentions and vibrations.

Now that your space is set and ready to go, it's time to make your journal.

# CREATING YOUR *shadow work journal*

In a lot of ways, your Shadow Work Journal is where your shadow work *lives*. It's where you will write out and process all of your prompts, analyzations, love letters, hate letters, and thoughts, as well as practice freewriting and anything and everything related to you and your shadow self. Think of it like a text chain between you, your shadow self, and your spirit guides. You ask the questions while they help you answer and figure it the fuck out.

Believe it or not, the journal itself is just as important as the words going into it. No, you don't need to buy an $80 journal with computing capabilities. I'm saying that whatever journal you do use needs to first be seasoned. How do we season a book? With intention. In this section, you'll prepare your shadow work journal by infusing it with magic, witchcraft, and your personal energy.

Let's begin with the outside. Grab some markers, paint, scissors, glue, old magazines, printed images, stickers—anything you want to use to decorate the front cover. I know it seems silly to add this as one of the steps but trust me, putting in effort to make this book yours will give you that boost of motivation to actually use it. There's no wrong way to decorate the journal because it's literally yours. I've made a list of some of the things I've used to decorate my journals throughout my practice, which I think will help y'all a lot.

## FABRIC COVERS

Fabric covers are perfect because they're super easy. Each type of material holds a different meaning. I tend to stick to leather or velvet. Velvet is linked to the element of water. Water corresponds to our emotions and intuition. Both are perfect for shadow work. Leather, on the other hand, is linked to earth. Earth corresponds to grounding and clarity, which is also fantastic for this purpose.

## PERSONAL SIGILS UNDER WAX SEALS

I've always said that sigils are just personal runes, and I mean that literally. Since sigils are so personal, creating your own makes the magic more potent. I recommend securing the sigils in place on the outer cover with a wax seal to "seal" your intention onto the journal. Try making sigils for words like "self-discovery," "introspection," or "emotional clarity." See page 33 for how to make a sigil.

## LAYERED PAPER OR COLLAGE

The ever-popular vison board technique works great in this setting. Cut out things that speak to you or represent you, or cut out shit that you enjoy. By layering them onto our journal, we're basically symbolizing the "layers" we go through in our shadow work to get to our shadow self.

## HANDPRINTS

Hands are significant in witchcraft—just look at palmistry. The whole practice was built around hands—and for good reason. Hands can tell us a person's emotional state, personality traits, and archetypes, and can even record significant life events. Adding your handprint is like adding your signature at the bottom of a paper—honoring your personal growth.

## BLACK SALT

Black salt is for protection, warding, and keeping shitty energy away. Try using super glue or hot glue to attach a sprinkle of black salt on the cover of your journal.

## MIRRORS

Craft mirror shapes are easy to find and perfect for your shadow work journal. Mirrors reflect truth and force you to face yourself.

## SANDPAPER

It's a literal reminder that shadow work is rough, but, in the end, the results shine.

## EYES

Eyes represent inner sight and intuition and reveal the hidden.

## PRESSED FLOWERS

These represent growth, beauty, and rebirth since flowers die every year and return like clockwork.

## FEATHERS (ethically sourced or synthetic)

Feathers represent freedom and lightness after heavy emotions come through.

## KEYS

What do keys do? They unlock doors. What does shadow work do? It unlocks your soul.

## SCRATCHED-IN SIGILS

Use an old pen or small knife to "carve" sigils onto your journal.

## MAP PIECES

Maps symbolize finding your way and having a guide.

## TWINE OR STRING

This symbolizes binding and holding your shit together.

Once your journal is fully decorated and ready to go, use the following ritual to infuse your magic into it.

# SHADOW WORK JOURNAL TRANSMUTATION RITUAL

**I DEVISED THE TECHNIQUE FOR THIS RITUAL MYSELF.** This is a transmutation spell that connects your journal to a talisman—in this case, a crystal spell jar—on your altar. Once you've identified the issue you're working through, your journal will communicate that to your talisman, which will, in turn, transmute the energy to something positive your subconscious can use to further develop your healing and shit.

**You'll need:**

A pen (bonus points for purple ink)

Shadow Work Journal

A small scrap of paper from your journal (use the last page so you don't noticeably damage it)

A jar or bag

Calendula

3 to 5 of the following in crystal chip form (if you don't have access to chips, use a bag or sachet instead of a jar so the crystals you do have can fit inside)

- Amethyst, for transmutation and self-awareness
- Obsidian, for transmutation and balance
- Labradorite, for transmutation and growth
- Fluorite, for transmutation and intuition
- Smoky quartz, for transmutation and grounding
- Carnelian, for transmutation and healing
- Selenite, for transmutation and clarity
- Clear quartz, for transmutation and renewal

A purple candle

First, draw your sigils. This will link your journal with your jar. Draw one sigil on the inside cover of your journal and the same sigil on the piece of scrap paper. If you're too lazy or tired to make your own, here is one of mine. Feel free to copy it.

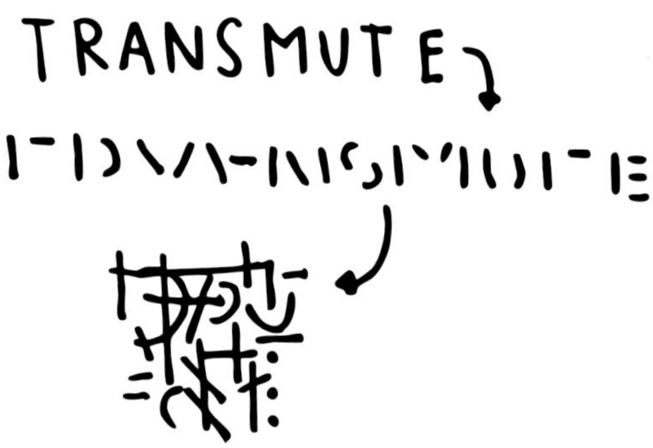


Add the scrap paper with the sigil to your jar. If necessary, use a pen to push it down to the bottom.

Next add your calendula. Place a pinch in the jar and another pinch on top of the sigil you drew in your journal. Next, add your crystal chips. Add a pinch of each one to the jar, and place a few pieces on your journal sigil all while telling them their jobs. You can use the intentions shown on the ingredients list. Once all of your crystals are in, seal the jar by dripping wax from your candle to completely cover all the spots on the cap/cork of your jar.

Close your journal with the calendula and crystal chips inside. Place your journal on your altar, and place the sealed jar right on top of that journal. Wave your hands over the journal and jar while chanting the following:

*Journal of wisdom, jar of light. Take my words, make them bright. Transmute the dark, let healing take its place. May clarity and growth take its place.*

Leave this set up on your altar overnight. In the morning, place the jar somewhere on your altar that won't need to be moved around too much. Recharge your jar in the moonlight every one to two months or as needed. Make sure to store your journal on your altar while it's not in use.

# USING YOUR *shadow work journal*

Now that your journal is fully activated, you're ready to start doing some shadow work. To that end, I've created a list of forty journal prompts to help you start meeting, and integrating, your shadow self.

Use your journal to answer the prompts in whatever order and however often you see fit.

These prompts have two parts. The first—the "what"—is essentially a deep question to get your mind working. The second—a "who, where, when, and why"—is to help you understand why you answered that question in that way. Answering prompts like this will help you navigate your triggers and help spot them BEFORE you react. This gives you the opportunity to adjust your reactions and strengthen your relationship with your shadow self.

The forty questions include a mixture of both magical and mundane prompts. The mundane prompts are general, geared toward identifying triggers and exploring uncomfortable emotions, etc. The magical prompts are specifically geared toward your craft.

A few things to remember before you begin. First, you do not need to do all these prompts at once. In fact, I highly advise against doing that. Each prompt is made to tackle a specific shadow trait or difficult experience, and we don't want to attack ourselves from every direction. That would be more like a police interrogation than a therapy appointment. Which brings me to my second point: You should only do one or two prompts per session, at least one or two times a month to start. Once you feel comfortable with the process, you can do it more often. Third, there is no "correct order" while going through this list. My favorite thing to do is close my eyes, let my finger glide along the page, and randomly stop. The prompt you stop on is the prompt you probably need to do.

## SHADOW WORK JOURNAL PROMPTS

**PROMPT 1: Identifying Triggers**
**Part 1:** What triggers me the most in others?
**Part 2:** Does this reveal something I might be avoiding in myself?

**PROMPT 2: Boundaries Are Hard**
**Part 1:** What boundaries do I struggle to maintain?
**Part 2:** What fear is stopping me from telling people to fuck off?

**PROMPT 3: Definitions and Preconceptions**
**Part 1:** What does the word "witch" mean to me?
**Part 2:** Where the fuck did I get that view?

**PROMPT 4: Come into Your Power**
**Part 1:** When do I feel the most powerful in my craft?
**Part 2:** What's stopping that feeling from happening every time?

**PROMPT 5: Uncomfortable Emotions**
**Part 1:** How do I usually cope with uncomfy emotions?
**Part 2:** Are those coping mechanisms healthy or harmful?

**PROMPT 6: Worth versus Unworthiness**
**Part 1:** When was the last time I felt unworthy?
**Part 2:** What story am I telling myself about my worth?

**PROMPT 7: Magical Tools**
**Part 1:** What magical tools do I rely on the most?
**Part 2:** Do I feel confident in my spells without these things?

**PROMPT 8: What I Want versus What I Deserve**
**Part 1:** What is something I want but don't feel I deserve?
**Part 2:** What is telling me that I don't deserve it?

**PROMPT 9: Manifestation Troubleshooting**
**Part 1:** What intention do I find hardest to manifest?
**Part 2:** What inner blockage might cause this?

**PROMPT 10: Defining Success**
**Part 1:** What is success to me?
**Part 2:** Whose definition am I really following?

**PROMPT 11: Black as It's Painted**
**Part 1:** How do I view curses or baneful magic?
**Part 2:** What bias do I hold, and where did it come from?

**PROMPT 12: Protect Yourself**
**Part 1:** What is my relationship to protective magic?
**Part 2:** Do I feel confident in the ability to shield myself?

**PROMPT 13: Finding Forgiveness**
**Part 1:** What is something I need to forgive myself for?
**Part 2:** Why can't I do that?

**PROMPT 14: Whoops, I Overreacted**
**Part 1:** When was the last time I overreacted?
**Part 2:** What deep wound was triggered in that moment?

**PROMPT 15: Intention Overextension**
**Part 1:** What intention do I overuse in my practice?
**Part 2:** Am I treating it as a quick fix or a tool for transformation?

**PROMPT 16: Different Strokes**
**Part 1:** How do I respond when seeing others practice differently from me?
**Part 2:** What does that reaction reveal about my magical insecurities?

**PROMPT 17: Me and My Anger**
**Part 1:** What is my relationship with anger?
**Part 2:** How do I express or suppress it?

**PROMPT 18: I Am My Own Worst Enemy**
**Part 1:** How do I self-sabotage?
**Part 2:** What fears or beliefs drive this shit?

**PROMPT 19: Self-Care Is Its Own Magic**
**Part 1:** What role does self-care play in my practice?
**Part 2:** How do I balance giving and receiving energy?

**PROMPT 20: Love Me, Love Me Not**
**Part 1:** When do I feel most unworthy of love?
**Part 2:** What experience is doing this to me?

**PROMPT 21: Thankful to Be a Witch**
**Part 1:** When was the last time I showed gratitude in my craft?
**Part 2:** How can I remember to do it more often?

**PROMPT 22: Avoiding Emotions**
**Part 1:** What emotion do I avoid the most?
**Part 2:** What do I believe will happen if I allow myself to fully feel it?

**PROMPT 23: Boundary Betrayal**
**Part 1:** When have I betrayed my own boundaries?
**Part 2:** Why do I think others' comfort matters more than my own?

**PROMPT 24: Speaker to the Dead**
**Part 1:** What fears do I hold around spirit communication?
**Part 2:** Are those fears mine or do they come from others?

**PROMPT 25: The Ghost of Failures Past**
**Part 1:** What failure haunts me the most?
**Part 2:** What meaning have I attached to that failure about my worth?

**PROMPT 26: Comparison Is the Enemy of Witchcraft**
**Part 1:** In which aspect of witchcraft do I compare myself to others the most?
**Part 2:** What is causing this low-key jealousy?

**PROMPT 27: Stop, I'm the Worst**
**Part 1:** What are the hardest compliments for me to accept?
**Part 2:** What story makes me fight against them?

**PROMPT 28: Magical Nerves**
**Part 1:** How do I handle fear when working with unfamiliar or new energies?
**Part 2:** What can I do to turn this fear into respect and trust?

**PROMPT 29: Lie to Me**
**Part 1:** When was the last time I lied to protect myself?
**Part 2:** What part of myself was I trying to shield?

**PROMPT 30: Good at This**
**Part 1:** How do I feel about my own abilities as a witch?
**Part 2:** What holds me back from fully embracing it?

**PROMPT 31: See Me**
**Part 1:** When do I feel the most invisible?
**Part 2:** What taught me that my presence wasn't important?

**PROMPT 32: Loving All of Myself**
**Part 1:** What part of myself feels the most unlovable?
**Part 2:** Where did I learn this part of myself was unacceptable?

**PROMPT 33: Love Is Not Currency**
**Part 1:** Who made me feel like I have to "earn" love?
**Part 2:** How does that show up in my current relationships?

**PROMPT 34: Give It a Rest**
**Part 1:** What is my relationship to magical rest or pause?
**Part 2:** When did I learn productivity = power?

**PROMPT 35: The Grudge**
**Part 1:** Who have I not truly forgiven?
**Part 2:** What would forgiveness give me that holding onto anger doesn't?

**PROMPT 36: Guilt Trip**
**Part 1:** What do I feel guilty about that wasn't really my fault?
**Part 2:** Who placed that guilt onto me?

**PROMPT 37: My Witchy Identities**
**Part 1:** What magical identities do I resist claiming (healer, seer, etc.)?
**Part 2:** What part of me doesn't feel worthy of that title?

**PROMPT 38: The Shame Spiral**
**Part 1:** What memories make me feel shame?
**Part 2:** How old was I when I learned to associate those memories with shame?

**PROMPT 39: Left Behind**
**Part 1:** When have I felt abandoned and rejected?
**Part 2:** How do I still carry that abandonment today?

**PROMPT 40: Finding What's Missing**
**Part 1:** What practices do I feel disconnected to lately?
**Part 2:** What shift in my energy is guiding that detachment?

# REFLECTING ON YOUR JOURNAL PROMPTS

So, you've started answering prompts. Now what the fuck do you do with those answers? You think. You sit. You reflect.

Here's an example straight from my own journal.

**Prompt:** What elements do I feel least connected to right now (air, fire, water, earth)?
**Answer:** I am the least connected to air at the moment.

**Prompt:** Is the loss of connection revealing something about my emotional state?
**Answer:** Well, air in witchcraft corresponds to clarity, inspiration, creativity, and freedom. Right now, I'm in the middle of making crystal altars for my drop, but my brain is getting foggy and my ideas aren't coming out like I want them to. I'm not connected because my clarity is at 0 percent, and I feel like I'm stuck in one spot.

If you're struggling to understand your answers, try the following approaches:

1. **Reflect on patterns and repetition:** This can be things like common triggers, reoccurring fears, insecurities, or doubts. This tells you where you need to focus your healing.
2. **Identify the root cause:** Ask yourself why you felt a certain way and what belief or life event made you feel like this. Understanding can help you release all the bullshit.
3. **Find opportunities for growth:** Locate areas you're confident or strong in, and compare those with areas where you have no faith in yourself. This perspective reminds you that you're not all shadow and you can work on things to help improve your life.
4. **Study your emotional responses:** What questions are easy to answer and get you excited as opposed to questions that make you sad or angry? This gives you "Where's Waldo?" level clues on what areas of your life push back the hardest and where you need to focus your healing.
5. **Connect craft to shadow:** How do your shadow traits show up in your witchcraft? Like, if you have issues with confidence, does this affect your ability to manifest? Making these connections helps you become a more *balanced* witch.

The point of shadow work is to recognize, not solve. You're not a fucking math equation; you're a human being. Ultimately, the goal is to integrate the emotions and stop pushing them down.

## THE ARCHETYPES

Carl Jung also gave us some cheat codes before he moved on to the next life. His list of twelve archetypes are universal patterns of human behavior and experiences that exist in our collective unconscious. The archetypes can function like "answers" to our prompts. They help identify reoccurring themes in your answers and give you a little push in the right direction when it comes to figuring out WTF to do about all the self-awareness you just acquired. Think of these archetypes as a road map to your subconscious. Refer to this list while you work through the prompts and see if you can connect your answers to certain archetypes. Once you can identify which archetype is linked to an answer, figuring out why you are the way you are and how to navigate that specific trait will come much easier.

**1 The Innocent: Purity, Hope, and Optimism**
The Innocent comes out when you're learning about your vulnerability and trust issues. Times when your optimism and hope have led to unrealistic expectations. We need to learn to trust ourselves and the world again. Try some affirmations that boost that hopefulness while still keeping those expectations within the realm of reasoning.

**2 The Orphan: Connection and Belonging**
The Orphan comes out when you're exploring feelings of abandonment and loneliness. Times when you feel lonely as fuck. We need to turn what we see as a weakness into a shared strength. Try having a get-together with some friends or join a community meet-up group (or a coven—a coven would be fire).

**3 The Hero: Courage and Determination**
The Hero comes out when you're dealing with arrogance and your ego. Times where you feel like you need to prove yourself or beat someone else. We need to balance our arrogance with a tad of humility. Try documenting your achievements and setbacks. Note what lessons are learned from both.

**4 The Caregiver: Nurturing and Compassion**
The Caregiver comes out when we do a lot of self-neglect and over-sacrifice—aka NOT DOING YOUR M-FING SELF-CARE. We need to give ourselves as much time and energy as we would give to others. Try—I don't know—maybe doing some self-care (insert stale face emoji here).

**5 The Explorer: Freedom and Adventure**
The Explorer comes out when dealing with the struggle to balance commitment issues and the need to feel rooted. We need to find the balance between adventure and stability. Try grounding exercises that help you balance your wanderlust with the need to be present in the moment, like walking through nature barefooted.

**6 The Rebel: Change and Transformation**
The Rebel comes out when rebelliousness turns into anger, chaos, and destructive behaviors for no reason. We need to channel that energy into transformation instead of destruction. Use movements like dancing or martial arts to transform your defiance into something with purpose and shit.

7 **The Lover: Passion and Intimacy**
The Lover comes out when you're dealing with emotions like obsession or codependency. We need to find a balance between passion and self-respect. Meditate on your past or present relationships, and write down qualities you think border on the obsession side. Then make another list of what a healthy, balanced relationship looks like to you.

8 **The Creator: Imagination and Expression**
The Creator comes out when reflecting on actions that show perfectionism or when creative blocks come up. We need to embrace these moments to get to that creative breakthrough. Try making a creative mini ritual to do before or while you create—something simple, like lighting an orange candle every time you draw or playing a specific song when you're writing.

9 **The Jester: Humor and Play**
The Jester comes out when you feel the need to cover up the fact that your world is on fire with humor and pretend nothing is wrong. We need to balance laughing with our pain rather than at our pain. Try laughter meditation where you literally just sit there and laugh—not like a padded white room type of laugh, but more like a laugh that's contagious.

10 **The Sage: Truth and Wisdom**
The Sage comes out when we explore the fear of being misled or ignorant. Times where your wisdom comes off as detached-from-reality arrogance. We need to balance intelligence with empathy. Try reading some witchy spiritual texts and reflect on how they can apply to your life.

11 **The Magician: Insight and Manifestation**
The Magician comes out when we're dealing with our own manipulative actions and unrealistic expectations in our manifestations. We need to balance overconfidence with the ability to turn our ideas into reality. Try dream journaling and analyzing those dreams to inspire your journey of transformation.

12 **The Ruler: Leadership and Responsibility**
The Ruler comes out when we're figuring out why we need to be in control of everything all the time like a tyrant. We need to figure out how to have compassion and authority at the same time. Try delegating (if you're like me, this is HARD). Let your roommate clean the coffee maker for once without micromanaging.

# OTHER WAYS TO USE YOUR SHADOW WORK JOURNAL

Your journal isn't necessarily just for answering the specific shadow work prompts in this book. You can—and should—use it for anything related to shadow work. For example:

**Free/Automatic Writing**
Let your intuition and spirit guides take over by clearing your mind and writing anything and everything that comes to your head. It doesn't need structure. Return to the page a few days later to see if you can find any hidden messages or advice.

**Dream Tracking**
Your dreams have a special front row view to your subconscious. When you have a dream, it's more than likely your higher being's way of saying, "YEAH, WE'RE FUCKING TALKING TO YOU." Jot down your dreams as soon as you wake up and make sense of the details at a later time.

**Letters That You'll Never Send**
For love, hate, anger, jealousy, or any other shadow emotions that aren't very "demure" to show in public, write those here. The world will never see them, but I'm sure you'll feel better after metaphorically screaming your lungs out. I've written to quite a few ex-boyfriends this way.

**Coloring Meditation**
Find a coloring book page or image online, print it out, and trace it into your journal. (If you can draw, well, you're lucky, and you should do that instead.) Match the drawing to your intention of the day and color it slowly for an intention-focused mini meditation.

**Shadow Spells**
Any shadow work–related spells you find in this book or anywhere else can be stored in your journal. This helps keep all your shadow work shit in one spot.

**Emotion Tracking**
Create a mini tracking table and use different colored markers to match each individual feeling. Track this for a month and take note how each day is connected or to see progress in your emotional stability.

Your journal should feel like a comfort object, not another dumbass checklist. Do whatever you feel is right in your soul and you'll be on the right track. That said, witchcraft gives us rituals that can guide us to improve certain areas. We can use these spells to help us heal and accept the experiences we uncover on our shadow work journey. That's what the next chapter is all about.

4

# shadow work SPELLS + RITUALS

The spells and rituals in this chapter are not here to replace your shadow work; they're here to support, enhance, and amplify it. Use them before an intense session, during a heavy emotional upheaval, or after a breakthrough—quite literally whenever you want. Do you have to do a ritual every time you pick up your pen? Absolutely fucking not. However, it's better to have the right spell and not need it than need it and not have it.

In this chapter, we'll go through spells and rituals that support and enhance our shadow work in two parts. The first part is linked directly to the moon and using her phases as a guide to enhance our understanding. The second part goes way beyond that, and is designed to support you before, during, and after your shadow work sessions.

But first, let's look at our shadow work correspondences.

# shadow work CORRESPONDENCES

I've created a list of eight intentions that we can use to infuse shadow work into our witchcraft and vice versa. These intentions are Introspection & Self-Awareness, Healing & Release, Growth & Transformation, Balance & Grounding, Clarity & Courage, Spiritual Connection & Intuition, Rebirth & Renewal, and Self-Love. I've also included a table for general shadow work correspondences for the times that you know you need something but don't exactly know what intention that would be. The ingredients in these tables will be used in spells and rituals throughout this chapter. You can also use them to create your own spells and/or substitute any herbs or crystals you don't have on hand.

## INTROSPECTION & SELF-AWARENESS

| Plants, herbs & flowers | Crystals & gemstones | Other shit |
|---|---|---|
| Angelica | Amethyst | **Color:** Lavender, purple |
| Calendula | Celestite | **Number:** 2, 7, 11 |
| Cedar | Labradorite | **Metal:** Silver |
| Chamomile | Lapis lazuli | **Tarot:** Hermit |
| Galangal root | Fluorite | **Element:** Water |
| Myrrh | Tiger's eye | **Zodiac:** Cancer, Scorpio |
| Sandalwood | Tree agate | **Day:** Wednesday |

## HEALING & RELEASE

| Plants, herbs & flowers | Crystals & gemstones | Other shit |
|---|---|---|
| Basil | Blue lace agate | **Color:** White, gold |
| Elderflower | Carnelian | **Number:** 1, 3, 7, 9 |
| Lavender | Celestite | **Metal:** Copper |
| Mullein leaf | Citrine | **Tarot:** The Sun |
| Rosemary | Moonstone | **Element:** Air, fire |
| St. John's wort | Moss agate | **Zodiac:** Aquarius, Scorpio |
| Yarrow | Tiger's eye | **Day:** Monday, Sunday |

## GROWTH & TRANSFORMATION

| Plants, herbs & flowers | Crystals & gemstones | Other shit |
|---|---|---|
| Calendula | Amethyst | **Color:** Purple, turquoise |
| Frankincense | Clear quartz | **Number:** 1, 3, 5, 7 |
| Juniper | Fluorite | **Metal:** Copper |
| Patchouli | Labradorite | **Tarot:** Death |
| Pine needle | Lapis lazuli | **Element:** Earth, water |
| Sandalwood | Moss agate | **Zodiac:** Aries, Leo |
| Yarrow | Amazonite | **Day:** Thursday, Sunday |

## BALANCE & GROUNDING

| Plants, herbs & flowers | Crystals & gemstones | Other shit |
|---|---|---|
| Angelica | Citrine | **Color:** Brown, green |
| Basil | Clear quartz | **Number:** 2, 6 |
| Frankincense | Fluorite | **Metal:** Iron, brass |
| Mullein leaf | Moss agate | **Tarot:** The Star |
| Myrrh | Obsidian | **Element:** Earth, air |
| Patchouli | Smoky quartz | **Zodiac:** Taurus, Libra |
| Sandalwood | Tiger's eye | **Day:** Wednesday, Friday |

## CLARITY & COURAGE

| Plants, herbs & flowers | Crystals & gemstones | Other shit |
|---|---|---|
| Basil | Carnelian | **Color:** Yellow, orange |
| Cedar | Clear quartz | **Number:** 1, 9 |
| Frankincense | Labradorite | **Metal:** Silver |
| Lavender | Lapis lazuli | **Tarot:** Strength, Star |
| Peppermint | Obsidian | **Element:** Fire, air |
| Rose | Selenite | **Zodiac:** Virgo, Pisces |
| Rosemary | Tiger's eye | **Day:** Tuesday, Thursday |

## SPIRITUAL CONNECTION & INTUITION

| Plants, herbs & flowers | Crystals & gemstones | Other shit |
|---|---|---|
| Birch | Amethyst | **Color:** Blue, violet |
| Frankincense | Clear quartz | **Number:** 7, 11 |
| Jasmine | Fluorite | **Metal:** Silver |
| Mugwort | Labradorite | **Tarot:** Hierophant |
| Rosemary | Lapis lazuli | **Element:** Air, water |
| Sandalwood | Moonstone | **Zodiac:** Pisces, Sagittarius |
| St. John's wort | Obsidian | **Day:** Sunday, Monday |

## REBIRTH & RENEWAL

| Plants, herbs & flowers | Crystals & gemstones | Other shit |
|---|---|---|
| Elderflower | Amethyst | **Color:** Brown, green |
| Lavender | Bloodstone | **Number:** 2, 4 |
| Lemon balm | Carnelian | **Metal:** Brass |
| Myrrh | Citrine | **Tarot:** Judgment |
| Patchouli | Clear quartz | **Element:** Earth, water |
| Rosemary | Selenite | **Zodiac:** Scorpio |
| Sandalwood | Tiger's eye | **Day:** Sunday |

## SELF-LOVE

| Plants, herbs & flowers | Crystals & gemstones | Other shit |
|---|---|---|
| Chamomile | Amethyst | **Color:** Pink, red, white |
| Elderflower | Carnelian | **Number:** 2, 3, 5, 6 |
| Galangal root | Clear quartz | **Metal:** Gold, Silver |
| Lavender | Garnet | **Tarot:** The Lovers |
| Rose hips | Lapis lazuli | **Element:** Fire |
| Rose petals | Moonstone | **Zodiac:** Cancer, Libra |
| Yarrow | Rose quartz | **Day:** Friday, Monday |

## GENERAL SHADOW WORK

| Plants, herbs & flowers | Crystals & gemstones | Other shit |
|---|---|---|
| Angelica | Amethyst | **Color:** Purple, blue |
| Basil | Fluorite | **Number:** 7, 8, 9 |
| Chrysanthemum | Labradorite | **Metal:** Iron |
| Lavender | Moonstone | **Tarot:** The Moon |
| Mugwort | Obsidian | **Element:** Water, earth |
| Nettle | Selenite | **Zodiac:** Pisces, Capricorn |
| Willow | Smoky quartz | **Day:** Monday, Saturday |

# shadow work & THE MOON

Did you know the moon doesn't actually produce light? It reflects light from the sun. Essentially, it's a mirror. So is shadow work. It reflects your shadow self onto you so you can truly see yourself. Because of this, linking shadow work with the phases of the moon is a no-brainer. The moon is going to amplify our emotions, feelings, and intentions, making the shadow work and spells much more powerful.

All of that being said, you do not need to do these rituals every cycle as if it's your electric bill on autopay. Nothing will happen if you skip a phrase or leave them out of a cycle—or never do them at all. Do them when you need to and when you want to.

We'll start at the beginning of the lunar cycle, with the new moon.

## ZERO-SPOON SHADOW WORK TIPS, SPELLS, AND RITUALS

**The following mini tips, spells, and rituals are super-easy, lazy witch–approved ways to regulate, soothe, deal with, and understand your emotions throughout your shadow work journey.**

- Write your negative thoughts on a bay leaf, and burn that shit to release emotions.
- Use a feather all over your body in a sweeping motion to "sweep away" heightened emotions.
- Rub your worries onto a candle and light it (physically rub the candle between your palms).
- Place amethyst near your bed to transmute emotions while you sleep.
- Use smoke from lavender or rosemary to clear emotional "heaviness."
- Scry into a bowl or mirror, and ask it to show your true emotions.
- Create an "emotion spill" sigil, hold it, and see what emotions arise.
- Carry a worry stone like obsidian or labradorite, and keep it in your pocket to calm wild emotions.
- Set your playlist to random, and see what songs appear. Then write in your Shadow Work Journal what you think the guides were trying to tell you with it.
- Sit in front of a mirror and have a conversation with your shadow self.
- Stir tea clockwise while stating self-soothing affirmations.
- Trace symbols and sigils into your palm for peace and clarity.
- Sleep with a sigil or rune under your pillow that signifies emotional stability.

# THE MOON SEED | A NEW MOON RITUAL

**THE NEW MOON IS THE TIME TO SET INTENTIONS** and work toward new beginnings. It's a perfect time to gather up all the parts of our shadow selves and ask the universe to guide us on our journey to healing. In this ritual, we'll basically be "rebirthing" our shadow traits by writing them out and asking (begging, TBH) the universe to help us heal that shit.

Sidenote: This spell is four spoons only because it requires going outside. I know, I hate leaving my house too. If you physically cannot leave your house, just do everything inside and use the "nonburial" closing.

**New Moon Intentions:** Intention setting, rebirth, new beginnings

**You'll need:**

Matches, for a stronger connection

1 white candle for new beginnings (see note)

A fireproof plate

Paper and pencil to set intentions (see note)

1 black candle for rebirth (see note)

Sandalwood, for renewal

Angelica, for introspection

Lavender, for healing

1 piece clear quartz for healing, rebirth, and renewal (optional)

Gather all your shit and go outside. Find a space where you won't be disturbed or burned at the stake.

With matches, melt the bottom of the white candle and stick it onto the middle of the plate. Close your eyes and take nine deep breaths. One, three, and nine are all numbers associated with new beginnings.

When you feel ready, write the shadow traits that you can remember on the paper. Usually, the ones you can remember or identify easily are the ones that need your attention the most.

Once your shadow traits are out in the open, cross them out, and write the traits you'd like to replace them with. For example, if my shadow trait is "anger," I'd cross that out and write "understanding" because I'm a hotheaded bitch who has ADHD and loses her shit at the smallest interruption when hyper-focused. I don't mean to; it's just the first reaction that comes out. It's not something I want to get rid of fully because some anger is healthy, but I'd like to replace the majority of it with something *better*.

Once you have listed all your new traits, fold the paper one time away from you to send the message out to the universe and twice toward you to bring that healing back to its rightful place.

*continued on page 76*

*continued from page 75*

Light the black candle and place it on the plate. Place the paper in front of the lit black candle. Scatter a few pinches of each of your herbs all over the plate and your folded paper. As you scatter them, say:

*With these herbs, my intentions are free. Healing flows through and within me.*

Let the wax from your white candle drip onto the paper. You want to cover the ENTIRE paper in candle wax. Please, for the love of everything holy and unholy, do not hold your candle too close to the paper or you'll start a fire.

As your candle drips (because that shit is going to take at least a full minute), repeat this chant as many times as you can until the paper is completely covered with candle wax:

*With this flame I embrace my healing, with this flame I bring in new beginnings.*

Once your paper is covered, blow out the white candle and keep it to the side as you wait for your black candle to finish burning. If you've opted to use the piece of clear quartz, place that on top of the wax sealed paper while you wait to add an extra layer of healing.

Once the candle is almost burned out (there should be about an inch left), blow it out. Yes, I said blow. The gods aren't going to curse you because you blew out a fucking candle. Remove the paper from the plate and bury it. Wherever. Doesn't matter. If for whatever reason you cannot bury it, put it in a container and cover it with salt. Leave it in the container for at least a week or until the new moon has passed.

**PRO TIP:**
**Bring your favorite coloring book outside with you so you're not just sitting there waiting. Bonus points for this because coloring is another form of meditation.**

**NOTE:**
**Please make sure the candles and writing utensils are biodegradable since you will be burying them. Soy, coconut, or beeswax candles are safe to bury.**

**BONUS NEW MOON ACTIVITY:**
**Create a "New Moon Intention" page in your journal by writing out your desired intentions for the month. Use the same page for each new moon to track your progress.**

# THE RISING MOON | A WAXING CRESENT SPELL

**THIS TEA RITUAL IS MEANT TO PREPARE YOU** for the shadow work you're about to do. The waxing crescent is all about courage and growth, so we're making a tea blend that brings confidence and courage before diving deep into your shadow work prompts.

**Waxing Crescent Intentions:** Growth, building, courage

**You'll need:**

8 to 10 ounces (235-285 ml) water in mug

1 teaspoon (2 g) nettle, for resilience

1 teaspoon (5 g) passionflower, for gentle courage

½ teaspoon cinnamon, for bravery

½ teaspoon cardamom or allspice, for motivation

1 teaspoon (3 g) rose petals, for emotional bravery

Tea strainer

Lemon and/or honey (optional)

Gather all the shit you need so you don't have to search your kitchen as you do this spell.

Heat up your water either on the stove or in the microwave. (I don't judge microwaved tea, okay?)

As your water heats up, place each herb in the tea strainer, one by one, while setting your intentions:

*I add this nettle for strength that never wavers.*
*I add this passionflower to get rid of self-doubt.*
*I add this cinnamon for brave action.*
*I add this cardamom for clarity and motivation.*
*I add these rose petals to open my heart with courage and strength.*

When your water is hot, add the strainer to the mug (or pour hot water over it if you boiled your water on the stove). Let the herbs steep for four to five minutes. You can leave it in longer for a more potent tea, but I already hate the taste of tea so I wouldn't. Add lemon and honey at this point if you'd like.

Sit down, close your eyes, and drink your tea, letting each sip fill your body with fiery courage. Then go do some fucking shadow work, bitch.

**BONUS WAXING CRESCENT MOON ACTIVITY: Light a candle and focus on building courage to face your shadows.**

# LUNAR FOCUS | A WAXING GIBBOUS SPELL BAG

**THIS PARTICULAR MOON PHASE** is the perfect time to make a spell bag for clarity. This bag will come in handy when you're going through and analyzing answers to your shadow work prompts from the last chapter. (I recommend analyzing one prompt at a time because, if not, you'll get overwhelmed, causing a foggy mind and defeating the purpose of this spell.) You won't see any intentions listed in the ingredients list, because they are all for clarity and focus.

**Waxing Gibbous Intentions:** Focus, clarity, refinement

**You'll need:**

A small indigo or white fabric bag

Basil

Peppermint

Rosemary

1 piece selenite

1 piece clear quartz

Small piece of paper

Pen

**BONUS WAXING GIBBOWUS MOON ACTIVITY:** Anoint yourself with a healing oil blend for emotional clarity, and then choose a prompt from your journal to review.

I'd make this on my altar space, but you can literally make it wherever, so grab all your shit and get into your zone.

As we add each herb to the bag, let's recite an affirmation.

Add basil and say: *I am clear on my purpose.*

Add peppermint and say: *I am clear on my goals.*

Add rosemary and say: *I am clear on my destiny.*

Add selenite and say: *I am clear on my soul.*

Add clear quartz and say: *My mind is focused.*

Now, take that scrap of paper and write out "Clarity" and "Focus." Then place it in the bag as well.

Once you've got all your shit in there, tie the bag shut as securely as humanly possible (or else herbs will start falling out, and we don't want that). Congratulations! Your bag is complete.

Whenever you're about to do some shadow work and feel like you need a little more clarity or focus, hold this bag in your hand and repeat the affirmations we listed above. This is how you'll activate the bag.

Once you're done with your shadow work, thank your bag for its service and leave it on your altar, preferably on a selenite charging plate. If not, you can charge it in the moonlight once a month to keep the energies strong.

# SELENE'S RELEASE | THE FULL MOON

**THE FULL MOON IS THE PERFECT TIME** to release everything you've uncovered about yourself through your shadow work (i.e., past traumas you've maybe not fully healed from but now realize don't define you anymore so why are they still hanging around?). You're more than welcome to do this spell indoors, but we will produce quite a bit of smoke, so please be mindful if you have sensitive nostrils and go TF outside if you must.

**Full Moon Intentions:** Release, truth, manifestation

**You'll need:**

A cauldron or fireproof bowl

4 tealight candles

Basil, for letting go

Sandalwood, for growth

Yarrow, for emotional healing

Mullein leaf, for spiritual release

1 piece moonstone, for lunar connection

1 piece labradorite, for transformation

1 piece clear quartz, for emotional release

1 piece amethyst, for spiritual healing

Lighter

¼ charcoal disk

Paper and pen

Place the bowl in the center of your workspace. Place the four tealights around the bowl, leaving the same amount of space between each one.

Next, add the herbs to the candles. When you're doing this, make sure the herbs don't fall close to any of the wicks. This causes larger flames and, well, fires. Let's not.

Take a pinch of basil and place it on one tealight and quite literally, out loud, say: *I let go.*

Add a pinch of sandalwood to the next candle and say: *I grow.*

Add a pinch of yarrow to the next candle and say: *I heal.*

Add pinch of mullein leaf to the last tealight and say: *I release.*

Next, we'll set up the crystals. The actual placement of each one doesn't matter as long as it's in between two candles (like, it doesn't have to be between specific candles).

Put the moonstone down and say: *I connect to the moon.*

Next, place your labradorite down and say: *I transform.*

Next, add your clear quartz and say: *I release,*

Last, add your amethyst, and say: *I heal.*

Light your charcoal disk, and place it in your cauldron. Sprinkle a pinch of each herb on top of the charcoal disk and get ready to write.

On your paper, write out all the negative shit you've discovered about yourself. Remember that this isn't a release where we'll get rid of those traits; it's about releasing them into the universe and giving yourself the peace of accepting and understanding it.

*continued on page 80*

*continued from page 79*

Once you've filled your paper or don't feel like writing anymore, it's time to rip that shit. Make sure you rip away from you, not toward you. We're releasing, not keeping.

I suggest using tweezers for this next part, but if you don't have any, just be extra careful not to touch the cauldron or charcoal. Place the ripped pieces of paper on the charcoal disk one at a time and let them burn fully. Once the paper is all burned, let the charcoal disk burn out and the cauldron cool slightly. Once you can pick the cauldron up without burning yourself, lift the cauldron to eye level, close your eyes, and say:

*I let it go, I let it free. I take a deep breath to release all that no longer serves me. The weight, the doubt, the fear, the pain—it washes away like summer rain. What is gone was meant to be. I let it go, I set it free.*

Take a deep breath and then blow the ashes out into the wind. Even if there's no wind—you get my point. You can sit here for a few moments and do some more breathing exercises. Then blow out your candles, say thank you to the moon, and go TF to bed.

**BONUS FULL MOON ACTIVITY: Take a bath with chamomile oils and dried herbs to cleanse emotional residue.**

# LUNAR REFLECTIONS | THE WANING GIBBOUS

**THE WANING GIBBOUS IS THE PERFECT TIME FOR A MIRROR** spell, to give us a chance to reflect on how far we've actually come in our journey.

**Waning Gibbous Intentions:**
Gratitude, reflection, acknowledgment

**You'll need:**
Lighter

Any kind of sandalwood-smelling candle or incense

A dry erase marker

A hand mirror (big enough to write on)

**BONUS WANING GIBBOUS MOON ACTIVITY:** Create a mini tea ritual to honor the shadow parts you've uncovered.

Light your candle or incense. Take a few deep breaths to let the scent fill your body and mind.

Next, with your dry erase marker, write down three things you're grateful for on the top part of your mirror. Here are some examples in case you're stuck on what to write:

- The present moment: being right here, right now, and all the possibilities that come with it.
- Lessons from the past: everything you've learned has led to a growth in wisdom and knowledge.
- Rituals and small joys: your favorite coffee, that cozy candle you bought.
- Nature: the warmth of the sun on your skin, the trees, the ocean, the smell of flowers.
- Your intuition: that inner voice that has never led you astray.
- People: supportive people in your life, family, friends, strangers.

Once you're done writing those, write three things you've learned on your journey. Here are some examples:

- Your shadow isn't evil; she just needed some love.
- Boundaries are protection spells for your mental health.
- Energy doesn't lie. If something feels off, it probably is.
- Shadow work never ends and each layer you work through brings you closer and closer to achieving your true higher self.

Sit in front of the mirror, close your eyes, and bow your head. Recite the following affirmation as many times as it takes for you to believe it:

*I honor my progress, I cherish my wisdom, I embrace my shadow.*

Leave the words on your mirror until the waning gibbous cycle is done. Erase and leave the mirror on your altar until it's time to do it again.

# MOON'S REST | THE WANING CRESCENT

**THIS MOON PHASE IS ONE OF MY FAVORITES.** It gives us a chance to chill the fuck out, breathe, and recover before starting the cycle all over again. With this spell, we're making an herb blend that can be used as an edible tea or a bath tea. If you hate baths, don't worry, I got you covered because, same.

**Waning Crescent Intentions:**
Rest, renewal, healing

**For both spells, you'll need:**
1 teaspoon (3 g) elderflower, for uplifting energy

1 teaspoon (2 g) chamomile, for calming and healing

½ teaspoon lavender, for stress relief

1 teaspoon (1 g) lemon balm, for emotional soothing

½ teaspoon yarrow, for inner strength

**For tea, you'll need:**
Tea strainer

Mug

8 ounces (235 ml) boiling water

Honey and lemon (optional)

**For the bath, you'll need:**
A bathtub

Bubbles (optional)

Lavender essential oil (optional)

**To Make the Tea:** Add the herbs to your strainer. Place the strainer in your mug, pour boiling water over, and let it steep for four to five minutes. Remove the strainer, discard your herbs, and add honey or lemon, if preferred.

Drink your while setting intentions in your head by repeating the following affirmations or making your own:

- *I give myself permission to rest.*
- *Resting is an act of love and restoration.*
- *With each new day, I step into a fresh beginning.*
- *I am a work in progress and that is a beautiful thing.*
- *My body knows how to heal; I trust its wisdom.*
- *I release pain and fear and make space for light and love.*

**To Make the Bath:** Make your tea according to the instructions above, but let it steep for eight to ten minutes to make it more potent. In the meantime, fill up your bath like you normally would. Add bubbles and essential oils if you'd like because why the fuck would you not? Pour in the steeped tea, and let it mix with the water. Sit in the tub while repeating the same affirmations as above.

Bonus points if you drink the tea while sitting in the tub (not the bathwater—I realize this sounds like I'm telling you to drink bathwater, but for the love of everything holy and unholy that is NOT what I mean).

**BONUS WANING CRESCENT ACTIVITY: Practice journaling without structure by writing down anything and everything that comes to mind to explore hidden feelings.**

# shadow work SUPPORT SPELLS & RITUALS

Digging into your shadow can be a lot. Sometimes you need a little extra support with motivation, intuition, or even just understanding what the fuck you wrote down. And that's where these spells and rituals come in to save the day. These tools are here to help support you before, during, and after your shadow work session. Each spell is labeled accordingly, along with the intentions it supports.

Quick note: The "after" spells in this section focus on sharpening intuition and divining messages. If you're looking for spells and rituals to help with recovery, aftercare, and self-care (and trust me, babe, you will need it), that's the whole third section of this book. Hang in there. It's coming.

# LIGHT & DARK TEALIGHT CANDLES

**LIKE I'VE VERY MUCH EMPHASIZED IN THIS CHAPTER,** shadow work isn't about fixing something that is broken, it's about accepting our shadow self as a super important part of what makes us who we are. For this spell, we need to dress a candle. Tealights are always my favorite for dressing because they make it so easy. Remember that adding herbs too close to a candle wick will cause a bigger flame than you want, so keep the herbs well clear of the wick.

**Intentions:**
Shadow work, self-acceptance, personal growth

**Shadow Work Phase:** During

**You'll need:**

Lighter or matches

2 tealight candles (see note)

Angelica, for acceptance

Galangal root, for introspection

Chrysanthemum, for general shadow work

A pinch of amethyst chips

This is a one-spoon spell for a reason: The method is super easy. Light your tealights, and let the top layer of the wax melt fully. This should take around three to five minutes. Once the tops of the candles are melty, blow out the flame.

Next, sprinkle a pinch of each herb onto the candle, keeping them away from the wick. Chant the corresponding affirmation while you add each herb individually.

Angelica: *I honor my shadow as my teacher, showing me where healing is needed.*

Galangal root: *I integrate my shadow, knowing it holds the key to my personal power.*

Chrysanthemum: *I allow myself to be seen, in both my brightest light and my darkest shadow.*

Last, sprinkle your amethyst chips onto the candles, and say:
*I am both the calm and the storm, the night and the dawn, the question and the answer.*

And that's it. Quite literally. To use them, light the candles every time you do shadow work, and repeat the chants while lighting them. Try placing them on both sides of your journal (left and right) while you work on some prompts.

**NOTE:** **Candle wax dries fast, so you'll need to read over the following steps before beginning the actual spell.**

# THE MIRROR'S SHADOW

**THIS SPELL IS PERFECT FOR WHEN YOU DECIDE** you want to be extra mean to yourself because your shadow revealed that maybe that "quirk" is actually not cute. Like, think about it. Would you let anyone talk to your best friend like you talk to yourself? What would you tell your friend? You'd tell them to get their shit together and not let anyone talk down to them, right? So why would you not treat yourself with the same compassion? We will fix that for you right now.

**Intentions:** Self-compassion, empowerment, transformation

**Shadow Work Phase:** Any time

**You'll need:**

Lighter or matches

A rose-scented incense cone or lightly scented candle

An incense cone holder

Shadow Work Journal

Pen

A small mirror

Sit on the floor, light your incense, place it in the holder, and take a few deep breaths to really get the scent into your soul. If you have asthma, use a lightly scented candle instead so you can breathe.

Start journaling all the negative traits you think you have or traits that have been reveled through shadow work. Once that list is done, stare at it and read it as if someone had written it about your sibling, your parent, your partner, or your best friend. Read it multiple times if you must.

On a new sheet of paper, write yourself a list of positive qualities that can be linked to the negative trait. Here are a few examples:

Negative trait: I yell when I get overwhelmed or stressed out.
Positive spin: My emotions flow through me so easily.

Negative trait: I shut people out when I'm upset.
Positive spin: I take time to process emotions to the fullest extent.

Negative trait: I struggle to ask for help.
Positive spin: I value my independence and abilities.

If it helps, you can write it like a love letter to yourself instead of just bullet points. When you've covered all the points from your first page, rip out that page, and throw it the fuck away. We don't want it.

Read each line of your second page to yourself while looking in the mirror and staring directly into your own eyes. Continue in this way until you've finished the entire list.

Breathe deeply for a few moments after you're done. Keep the mirror on your altar for three days. Repeat this spell whenever your shadow work feels like it's punching you in the face.

# DEPTHS REVEALED BATH RITUAL

**THIS IS FOR MY BATH WITCHES.** This mini ritual is best done before you begin your shadow work. It will help us open our minds, bringing clarity, which, in turn, will help us identify, accept, and heal our shadow selves. The warmth of the water in your tub symbolizes the opening of the mind, just like the water opens our pores on "full bath" day. If you know, you know.

**Intentions:** Shadow work, clarity, wisdom, strength

**Shadow Work Phase:** Before

**You'll need:**

A bathtub

Rose petals, for wisdom

Basil, for strength

Calendula, for self-awareness

4 pieces blue lace agate, for clarity and healing

Lavender oil, to link the spell to general shadow work (see note)

Start by filling the tub. As it's filling, gather your ingredients. I suggest turning on some music to vibe to or lighting a few candles to set the mood. Be sure to bring this book with you—just don't drop it in!

Once the tub is filled, add your herbs. Make sure you're adding them in a clockwise motion to bring all of this energy deep into your soul.

Start by adding your rose petals. Say: *Ancient wisdom, clear and bright. Open my eyes, give me second sight.*

Next, add a bit of basil and say: *Let my fears go silent and my truth grow vibrant.*

Last, add your calendula and say: *Yellow flowers shine within, help me see where I begin.*

Pick up your blue lace agate. Hold all of the pieces in both hands and say: *Stone of calm, clear my sight. Bring my shadows to the light.* Then place one piece in each corner of your bathtub.

We'll use lavender oil to tie in all the shit we just did. Pour a little in your bath and say: *Spell is started, spell is linked, shadow work is ready to begin.*

Now get in that damn bathtub and fucking relax. Close your eyes, take some deep breaths.

Breathe in for six counts, hold for four counts, release for seven counts. Do this at least three times.

Visualize your shadow self in front of you. What does she look like? What color hair does she have? What color eyes does she have? Does she have any tattoos or birthmarks? Is she wearing something specific? Getting to know your shadow is key to stopping that fear we have when those emotions arise.

After that, you can continue to enjoy your bath. I'd recommend staying in for at least ten minutes, but that's totally up to you.

Once you're all done, drain the water, clean the tub, and say: *Spell is complete, spell is done, shadow work starts, the truth shall come. Mind is open, heart is clear. I face my shadow with strength, not fear.*

Go on to have a nice cup of tea and a successful shadow session, my children.

**NOTE: Substitute lavender oil with rose oil if allergic to lavender.**

# HIDDEN TRUTHS HERB BLEND

**SOMETIMES (WELL, AT LEAST FOR ME)** doing shadow work can feel like extracting teeth with rusty pliers in the middle of summer in Atlanta. We don't want to be stuck on one prompt for three hours though; we want to make this as smooth as possible so that shadow work doesn't feel like a whole-ass errand we have to run at Walmart. This herb blend can be used as incense, as tea blends, or as candle dressings. And guess what? We're about to do all of that.

**Intentions:** Exploring emotions, intuition, balance

**Shadow Work Phase:** During

**You'll need:**
8 ounces (235 ml) boiling water in a mug

1 teaspoon (7 g) yarrow, to deal with, support, and understand emotions

2 teaspoons (3 g) chamomile, for balance and grounding

1 teaspoon (3 g) mugwort, for intuition and spiritual guidance (see note)

1 teaspoon (1 g) lavender, for emotional balance

2 teaspoons (2 g) lemon balm, for processing emotions more easily

A normal bowl

Tea strainer

A blue chime candle

Lighter

A cauldron or fireproof bowl

1 piece clear quartz, for amplification

Lemon and honey, to taste (optional)

First, gather all of your shit. You can leave the mug in a microwave to keep it hot while you do the rest of the ritual first.

Let's make the herb blend. Combine all of your ingredients one by one in your "normal bowl." As you add each, repeat the corresponding chant.

Yarrow: *I release stress and allow my emotions to flow freely.*

Chamomile: *I allow myself to heal at my own pace.*

Mugwort: *I allow my guides to lead me through my journey.*

Lavender: *I find balance between my light and shadow.*

Lemon balm: *I welcome peace and clarity into my heart.*

Mix your herbs with your finger, not a spoon, to infuse your personal energy.

Place half of the mix in the tea strainer. Set the second half aside. Add the strainer to your mug, and allow it to steep for five to eight minutes. While its steeping, set up the next part.

Roll your chime candle in the second half of the mixture. You can heat up the candle with a lighter by passing the candle through the flame, but it's not completely necessary. We just want the energy—the essence, if you will—to stick to the candle.

Melt the bottom of the candle slightly, and stick it in the middle of your cauldron. Add the remaining herbs from the half mixture to the cauldron around the base of the candle. Light your candle and hold the piece of clear quartz in your hand while saying:

*Universe large and true, help me uncover what has been moved. All that is hidden is revealed, handled with care, not fear. Let my emotions flow through the pen onto the page; let those emotions balance me with grace. As it is done, as it shall be. No more shadows hidden beneath.*

Your tea should be done steeping at this point. Add the optional lemon and honey and drink your tea while beginning a shadow work prompt. Let the candle burn all the way down, and let the herbs at the bottom catch fire.

Once you're done and everything has cooled down, discard the remnants of the spell in a trash can located outside of your home.

**NOTE: Please note that mugwort is harmful when taken in large doses or if you are pregnant or breastfeeding or have certain medical conditions that can cause adverse reactions. Please research and make sure it's safe for you before consuming. If it is not for you, substitute with jasmine.**

# THE SPIRIT TEA

**WHEN YOU'RE UNCOVERING SO MUCH HIDDEN DIRT** and trauma in your shadow work, you can possibly start to doubt yourself, your guides, and your intuition. This tea counteracts that. Drink it after a tough session to strengthen intuition and call in guidance when you don't trust yourself or the answers you're getting.

**Intentions:** Intuition, spiritual connection, clarity

**Shadow Work Phase:** After

**You'll need:**

½ teaspoon mugwort (see note), for spiritual connection and psychic abilities

½ teaspoon cinnamon, for awareness and to open your mind to messages

Tea strainer or bag

8 ounces (235 ml) hot water in a mug

1 piece fluorite, to connect to the astral realm

1 piece labradorite, to contact spirits

1 piece amethyst, to clear the mind of outside thoughts

Vanilla extract, for focus (optional)

Dash of almond milk, for wisdom (optional)

Honey, for a touch of healing energy (it also cancels out the bitterness of the mugwort) (optional)

Tarot cards or preferred form of divination

First, prepare your tea blend. Add the mugwort and cinnamon to your strainer or tea bag. As you add them in, tell them what they're doing there using the intentions listed in the ingredients list. Seal the strainer or bag, and put it to the side.

Place your cup of hot water wherever you're doing the spell. Place your crystals in a triangle around (but not touching) the mug. Place your tea bag or strainer in your hot water. Recite this chant:

*Spirit hear me, universe as one. Connect to me now, let the veil be undone. Only my guides can enter this space, all other spirits please stay away. Guide me on my journey, open my eyes, so I may see what's hidden and uncover self-told lies.*

Let the tea steep for three to four minutes. The longer you leave it, the more potent the taste. Mugwort tastes like shit, unfortunately, but it is such a powerful herb for divination that we use it regardless. Kind of like coffee.

Once the tea is done brewing, remove the bag and discard it in the trash. Add in the vanilla, milk, and honey, if you wish. Use the intentions in the ingredients list while adding these as well.

When preparing to take your first sip, close your eyes and visualize a glowing, indigo light coming from your third eye. Drink your tea. When you feel ready, grab your tarot cards or divination tool of choice, and ask the following questions:

1. What does my healing path look like?
2. What steps can I take to help my healing?

You can keep going and ask as many questions as you need to figure this shit out, but remember: Divination is all about interpretation. Don't lose your shit if the answers are straight up yes or no. Sit with each answer and see what you can uncover.

**NOTE: Please always look up the effects of mugwort before consuming to make sure it doesn't interfere with medications or conditions. Do not drink while pregnant or breastfeeding.**

# LISTEN UP, BITCH

**DURING SHADOW WORK,** we rely heavily on the guidance of our divine helpers and guides. Sometime, spirit guides send really subtle messages, but we're usually so busy or tired that we miss them completely. It's not that your intuition is MIA, it's just that today's world doesn't give us much room to breathe. This bag is going to anchor your intuition and let you take it with you wherever you go. This way you can continue to receive messages from the guides even outside of active sessions, whenever or wherever you are.

**Intentions:** Intuition, spiritual connection, clarity

**Shadow Work Phase:** After

**You'll need:**

Mugwort, for spiritual connections

Damiana, for intuition and attraction

Rosemary, for alignment and self- and spatial awareness

Jasmine, for psychic ability and communication

Sandalwood essential oil, for third eye activation

A small mixing bowl

A small spoon or scoop

Small satin, velvet, or cotton bag (bonus points if it's purple or violet)

Small jar with cork

A pinch of amethyst chips plus 1 amethyst tumble, for spiritual contact

A pinch of labradorite chips plus 1 labradorite tumble, for psychic clarity

2 small pieces of paper and a pen

Start by mixing all of the herbs and oil in the bowl. There are no measurements for this spell because it's up to you and the size of the container you chose. The amounts don't have to be equal—amounts won't affect the spell either way. Once you've added the sandalwood, use the spoon to mix it all together. As you mix, repeat this chant as many times as you want (minimum of three):

*Guide my hands and align my sight. Wake my soul and clear my light. With every stir, the veil grows thin. Let spirit's voice be clear within.*

Place one scoop of the mixture in your bag. Place the rest of the mix in your jar. We're using the jar as our anchor, which will be left on our altar, and the bag as our portable lifeline.

Next, hold your amethyst tumble and chips in your hands. Say: *With amethyst, I clear the line; messages flow divine not mine.* Place the tumble in the bag and the chips in your jar.

Last, hold the labradorite tumble and chips in your hands. Say: *Let labradorite ignite the spark and light what once was dark.* Then place the tumble in the bag and the chips in your jar.

Grab your papers and pen. On one piece of paper, draw an empty circle. Place that in your bag. This is the receiver. On the second paper, draw a filled-in circle. Place that in your jar. This is the sender.

Seal your bag and close your jar. Hold them both in your hands and say: *One to anchor, one to roam. Spirit speaks wherever I go.*

Place the jar on your altar, preferably next to your tarot cards or your preferred method of divination. Keep the bag in your purse or pocket.

Use this spell when you feel disconnected from your intuition, when you're asking for signs and not getting them, or when you feel like your magic is on mute.

# shadow work
# TAROT CARD SPREADS

Shadow work is about finding what's hidden, and that's exactly what tarot cards do. So why the fuck would we not put them together? Think of the cards as your therapist in this moment. They're not there to simply *answer questions*, they're there to help you reflect on what is uncovered. Whether you need help breaking down a journal prompt, figuring out the next step, or just getting a quick vibe check, the cards have you covered. The spreads in this next section are like the gateway drug to creating your own spreads. Just focus on your question while you shuffle, lay out out the cards in the order listed, and let the universe do its thing.

## SPREAD 1: PAST, PRESENT, AND FUTURE

This spread is for analyzing how your past, present, and future can give you insight on why you are the way you are (and how to stop if it's not serving a higher purpose).

1. What am I repressing?
2. What the fuck caused this?
3. Advice from the guides on how to not do that shit.

## SPREAD 2: LET THE SHADOW DECIDE

This spread will give you a starting point on days when you don't know where to begin with your shadow work or how to work through certain prompts you're stuck on.

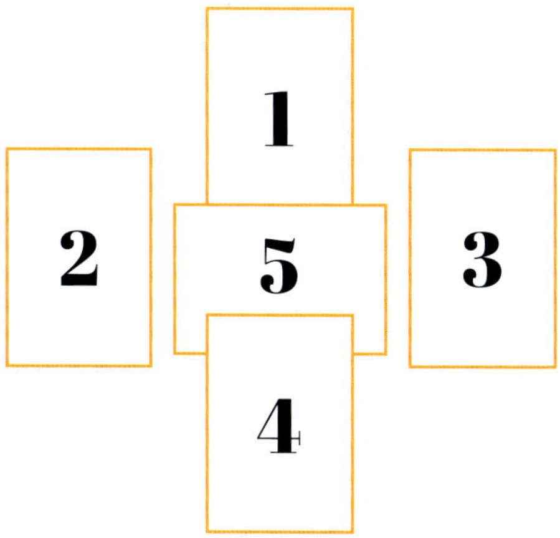


1. What shadow part wants to be recognized today?
2. How has it been affecting my life?
3. What is that shadow part trying to show me?
4. How do I incorporate it into my nonshadow side?
5. What can I finally release today?

## SPREAD 3: THE SIMPLE PULL

For this one, you need to shuffle continuously until your intuition tells you to stop. Once that happens, choose a card from your deck. Just the one. Meditate on this card and its message. You can make notes about it in your journal using the following prompts:

- What card was it?
- How does it make you feel (with no bias)?
- Does this card show up regularly?
- If this card were your friend or mentor, what would they say to you?
- What does this card make you think about yourself?

Write down your findings and repeat the pull one week from now with the same intention in mind while you shuffle. Consider:

- Did you pull the same card?
- If yes, ask yourself whether you've actually been taking the advice from your last pull.
- If not, what's different about the tone?

See? Wasn't that easy? Shadow work and shadow support aren't meant to be hard, complicated, or fucking annoying, but, when it is, we have our guides to get us through it. However, you can't just tear up your soul like that and walk away. Now it's time to care, comfort, and slowly rebuild ourselves with some shadow work aftercare.

# PART 3

# shadow work SELF-CARE + AFTERCARE

Shadow work is a bitch of a process. You work through your trauma, identify triggers, and explore a lot of things that you probably didn't want to think about. This not only makes you low-key relive the trauma, but it also throws your nervous system out of whack when you're constantly digging this deep and never taking care of yourself afterward.

It is absolutely crucial to create an aftercare plan to help your nervous system say, "Hey! That was a fucking lot, but you're done now. It's okay, you can rest." When we neglect ourselves after shadow work, we leave an open wound. And what happens to open wounds with no care? Infection—negative thought patterns—and bleeding—constant overthinking, anxiety, and worry.

In this section, I'll give you spells and rituals that are meant to take care of your mind, body, and spirit after a shadow work session. This way, you get to pick and choose exactly which spell works for you and which spells you're capable of (and willing to do) after each session. I won't create your aftercare plan for you, but I will give you more than enough tools to create your own routine. Use what resonates, ignore what doesn't (or just save for later), mix-and-match, and make it your own. You already did the hardest part; now it's time to take care of your soul.

5

# incense, teas + HERB BLENDS

Herbal blends, including teas and incense, are staples of the witchy community. These blends represent all four elements: earth (herbs), fire and air (when burned), and water (when brewed). They have been used for centuries across multiple cultures, from ancient Greece and Egypt to Indigenous and folk traditions, for healing, offerings, rituals, and general power. In this chapter, we'll go over blends that help us care for ourselves after an intense shadow session.

Before we begin, I have some notes for you. First, and most importantly, if you hate teas (like me—I know, blasphemous), make it into a lemonade instead. Brew the tea however the spell calls for, let it get cold in the fridge, and add lemon juice and sugar. That's it: magic lemonade. Tea isn't for everyone (trust me, I've tried), but lemonade is usually the move.

All teas and incenses are herb blends, but NOT ALL HERB BLENDS ARE TEAS OR INCENSES. In other words, not all herb blends are meant to be ingested or inhaled. Please, for the love of everything holy and unholy, research your herbs. If you're pregnant or breastfeeding, please consult with your doctor before ingesting or inhaling anything.

Now, let's brew a cup of comfort.

# CUP-OF-THERAPY FOR RELEASE

**THIS BLEND IS ALL ABOUT PROCESSING FEELINGS** without judgment and releasing all self-doubt and negative self-talk to achieve emotional balance. We forgive other people for saying mean things all the time, but have we ever forgiven ourselves?

**You'll need:**

½ teaspoon lavender, for healing and compassion

1 teaspoon (3 g) rose petals, for release and confidence

1 tablespoon (5 g) chamomile, for inner peace and emotional security

1 tablespoon (21 g) yarrow, for balance and happiness

Strainer or tea bag

8 ounces (235 ml) hot water in mug

A hand mirror

Tissues (optional, but, trust me, you'll want them)

Start by brewing your tea like you normally would. Add the herbs to the strainer, then steep in the mug of hot water; remember to set your intentions, as shown in the ingredients list, as you add each herb to the strainer or tea bag.

Sit in a cozy, comfy space and hold the cup in your hands. Close your eyes and say, *I am allowed to cry, I am safe with myself. I give myself permission to feel.* Drink about half the tea before moving on to the next step.

When you're ready, grab your mirror and hold it up to your face. Say the following affirmations, repeating each one as many times as you need to believe it.

- *I am not broken.*
- *I am enough.*
- *I am worthy.*
- *I am perfect exactly as I am.*
- *I am growing and becoming.*
- *I am here for a purpose.*
- *I am deserving of rest.*

Once you're done, drink the rest of your tea. When the cup is empty, say: *I am enough, I am enough, I am enough.*

Blot your eyes with your tissues. Rinse your glass, and maybe curl up on the couch and watch your favorite movie.

## ONE-SPOON SHADOW WORK AFTERCARE TIPS & TECHNIQUES

Full spells and rituals are great, but here are some super short, super simple, one spoon shadow work aftercare techniques that you can do whenever and wherever you are.

- Stretch: Stretching creates movement, and movement releases stress both physically and spiritually.
- Enjoy Your Favorite Beverage: Treat yourself to a glass of your favorite drink, whatever that might be. Since it's your favorite, your body and mind will associate it with comfort, which will help ease anxiety.
- Grab a Blanket: Wrapping yourself in a blanket applies pressure and gives your body the sensation that you're being hugged, which creates a sense of safety.
- Use the 5-4-3-2-1 Method: This is often used for anxiety and panic attacks. Here's how it works: Name five things you can see, four things you can hear, three things you can touch, two things you can smell, and one thing you can taste. This method grounds you and brings you back to the moment when you're stuck in your thoughts.
- Touch Grass: I mean this literally. Touching grass connects you back to the earth and grounds you.
- Use Oils: Oils are perfect because they're portable. Choose an oil from chapter 2 to keep in your pocket, car, or backpack, and dab it on your wrists throughout the day to remind you to be nice to yourself.
- Wash Your Hands: This is a perfect time to use the handwashes from part 1 to cleanse your body of any negative self-talk and residual gunky energy.
- Try 5-4-5 Breathing: Here's how it works: Breathe in for five seconds, hold it for four seconds, breathe out for five seconds. Doing this cycle three times helps your nervous system remember that you are not, in fact, being attacked—you're just stressed.
- Drink Water: Drink a full glass of water to rehydrate those tears you lost and bring awareness back to your body.
- Watch Your Comfort Shows: Comfort shows are shows that you keep rewatching (my favorite is *Supernatural* or *Grey's Anatomy*). Since you've seen the show a million times, you know exactly what's going to happen. This gives your body the sense that it's back in control and distracts you from whatever spiral was about to go down.
- Stand in the Sun: The sun is the source of all of our power and is connected to happiness and vitality. Standing outside in the sun for two minutes brings that warmth back into your body and helps your brain get some fresh air.

# CROSS-THE-LINE CHAI

**FEAR OF FAILURE IS A SHADOW EMOTION** that comes up quite a bit when we're working through unprocessed trauma. This tea is meant to counteract those fears. It will help you step outside of your comfort zone so you can grow and reach your full potential.

**You'll need:**
A chai blend (premade because it's so much easier)

A floor and wall

1 piece tiger's eye, for confidence and courage

Prepare your tea like normal. Pro tip: The ready-to-drink chai blends give off the same energy and save you the trouble of brewing.

Sit on the floor with your tea with your back against the wall and legs fully extended. This will anchor your aura (the energetic vibrations your soul naturally gives off). No crisscross applesauce, or it will disrupt the flow.

Place the tiger's eye in between your feet on the floor. Hold the tea close to your face so you can smell the aromas. Close your eyes and visualize roots growing from your feet into the ground. Then imagine white lights shooting up through the roots and going into your body. This is your strength rising up.

Open your eyes and take your first couple of sips. Then, it's time for a pep talk. You can adjust or make up your own, but here's one that I use on myself:

*Listen up, you beautiful-ass bitch. You were built to tackle the world. You were never meant to sit quietly and patiently wait your turn on the sidelines. You can do this. You are doing this. I believe in you.*

Drink the rest of your tea, and do the damn thing.

# RELEASE-THAT-SHIT INCENSE

**YOU'RE NOT REQUIRED TO CARRY YOUR EMOTIONAL BAGGAGE.** You're carrying unnecessary weight and heavy feelings wherever you go, and it's making it harder for you to exist. This incense helps you let go of the pain you've already survived so you can move on with your life.

**You'll need:**
1 tealight candle

Moonstone chips, to unite mind, body, and spirit

Pen and paper

Heat-safe dish or spoon

1 part birch bark, for new beginnings and security

1 part comfrey, for balance and strength

2 parts rosemary, for rebirth and release

2 parts frankincense, for blessings and banishing

Lighter or matches

Place your tealight in the center of your workspace. Sprinkle a small amount of your moonstone chips on and around the tealight, directly onto your workspace, making sure to keep them away from the wick. Say: *Moon connection and lunar light. Let my mind, body, and spirit unite.*

Next, write down whatever you wish to release on the paper. You can do this by either writing a short, bullet-point list or writing an intricate letter to yourself. Once you're done, fold the paper once away from you and stick it underneath your tealight.

In your heat-safe dish or spoon, add in a pinch of each herb according to their measurements. For example, one part birch bark is one pinch. Two parts rosemary is two pinches, and so on.

As you add them to your dish, just think of each herb's intention. No need to say it out loud.

Light your tealight and let your dish or spoon hover on top of the candle. The heat should start smoldering the herbs. Be careful if you're using a dish. The flame will 100 percent heat up the bowl and might burn your fingers if you leave it there too long. Just pay attention to the warmth of the vessel. Once the herbs are smoldering, say: *Herb and smoke, my intent is release. Take all that I've written and let it cease. I let go of what does not serve me and make space for what holds me gently.*

Close your eyes and visualize the words flying off the paper and going up in flames.

Once you're done, discard the herbs and cleanse the dish. Throw the paper of things you released in a trash can outside of your home. Alternatively, you can burn or bury the paper. It's totally up to you!

# CREATIVE OPENING INCENSE

**THIS INCENSE IS FOR WHEN YOU FEEL DISCONNECTED** from things that used to bring you joy. Shadow work can cause us to spiral and forget who the fuck we are, so this blend is designed to help you reconnect with hobbies and passions that you might have forgotten about while you've been processing your shit.

**You'll need:**

A 1-ounce (28 ml) jar

1 part rose petals, for confidence, grace, and inner power

1 part cinnamon, for creativity, harmony, and inspiration

1 part damiana, for passion and reignition

A lighter

A charcoal disk

A fireproof dish or cauldron

We'll start by adding the herbs to the jar. Fill the jar about one-fourth of the way with rose petals, and say: *Rose, give me confidence and inner grace. Let my courage take me back to my sacred place.*

Next, add your cinnamon, filling another one-fourth of the jar. Say: *Cinnamon, inspire me to do what I love. Let my creativity fit me like a glove.*

Finally, add your damiana, filling another one-fourth of the jar, and say: *Damiana, drive my passion. Ignite the flame. Push me to action.*

Cap your incense jar and hold it in both hands. Say: *I bless this blend with imagination and whimsy. My creativity flows through me easily. My happiness returns with grace and love. With this shake, the spell is done.*

Now shake the absolute fuck out of that jar to combine everything. This is the perfect blend to use before doing anything creative or while brainstorming what you should do to distract yourself from the shadows of shadow work.

To use the incense: Place a lit charcoal disk in your fireproof dish. Sprinkle a little bit of your loose incense on top. Repeat some affirmations, and get started on whatever project you're working on.

# SUNSHINE IN A FUCKING MUG

**PERFORM THIS MINI TEA RITUAL IN THE MORNING** to start your day with joy and warmth. This tea blend is designed to lift your mood and soften emotional baggage so it's not too heavy to carry. We'll also use it to charge a crystal with the same intent, so you can carry the vibes with you all day. This is an especially good ritual for days after heavy shadow work sessions because you're basically hitting a reset button on your feelings.

**You'll need:**

8 ounces (235 ml) hot water in mug

2 tablespoons (14 g) calendula, for solar energy and happiness

1 tablespoon (2 g) lemon balm, for comfort and healing

1 teaspoon (1 g) peppermint, for clarity and creativity

½ teaspoon hibiscus, for peace and blessings

Wildflower or regular honey, to taste and sweeten intentions

A citrine bracelet, ring, or regular crystal

Start by brewing your tea. I usually don't use a bag or strainer for this blend because I like how the vibes feel when the herbs are free floating. It feels more liberated. Simply add to hot water all of the herbs while telling each one what they're there for.

Add your honey, and stir clockwise because we want all of that energy to come into our bodies, minds, and souls. Think about something you're looking forward to while you do this. Place your mug on a windowsill or outside to charge for four to six minutes. If you're charging outdoors, put a napkin on the cup so you don't get bugs and shit in there because that would be bad.

Once your tea is charged, drink it while holding your citrine bracelet, ring, or crystal. Imagine the tea flowing through your body and flowing into the crystal.

Finish your tea and wear or carry your citrine for the rest of the day. It should stay charged for a week, so you'll need to redo the spell after that time if you wish.

**NOTE: If you don't like tea, this is a great blend to turn into a lemonade.**

# DREAM BURRITO

**DO YOU EVER HAVE MOMENTS** where you think your intuition is trying to tell you something, but you can't hear it because your brain won't shut the fuck up? This incense will clear all the noise and open your dreams up to messages, clarity, and subconscious unpacking.

**You'll need:**

1 part mugwort powder, for spiritual connection and clarity

2 parts sandalwood powder, for wisdom and psychic ability

1 part mullein leaf powder, for nightmare removal and balance

1 part lavender powder, for peaceful dreams and blessings

Small mixing bowl

Spoon

Natural paper (around 2 by 3 inches [5 by 7 cm]), such as unbleached rice paper

A soft, graphite pencil

An ashtray or ash catcher

1 piece amethyst, for prophetic dreams and spiritual protection

A lighter

Before we start, I want to emphasize that we ARE NOT smoking this. I repeat: DO NOT SMOKE THIS. We're simply using it as a vessel to make it into a makeshift incense stick.

First, combine all your powders in a small bowl and mix them together with a spoon. Stir clockwise because we want to bring those messages to us.

Next, take your natural paper and pencil and use the words "spirit, dream, message" to create a combined sigil on the paper (see page 33 for how to create a sigil).

Once that's done, it's time to roll. Think of this step like rolling a tiny little burrito. Lay your paper flat and horizontal in front of you. Use your spoon to scoop a small amount of the powder mixture onto the paper, down the middle, in a straight line. Don't add too much or it'll be harder to roll. Gently (meaning don't crease the paper) fold one long side of the paper over the herbs and then tuck and roll it into a burrito shape. Then twist the ends so the powder doesn't have a chance to fall out.

Take your ash catcher to your bedroom. Around twenty to thirty minutes before bed, place the piece of amethyst in the catcher and light your burrito. Waft the smoke around the room until the smoke seeps into every corner. You can leave your burrito in an ash catcher and let it burn out (only do this if you're not immediately going to sleep) or just put it out and save it for next time.

Before you close your eyes while in bed, say: *The wisdom I seek will appear in my dreams. My spirits guide me as I sleep. Bring messages and insight on the problem at hand. My ancestors protect me while I am sleeping.*

**PRO TIP:** Keep a dream journal next to your bed. As soon as you wake up, write down everything and anything you can remember. Revisit it after you've had your morning coffee to decipher anything you need.

# PROCESSING-THE-BULLSHIT INCENSE

**THIS RITUAL IS FOR WHEN A SHADOW WORK PROMPT MAKES YOU PAUSE.** When a question is so raw, you shut down or feel too much. This is for times when your emotions are screaming so loud, you almost can't focus on what they're saying. The smoke will soften the edges around your emotions so you can get to what it is you need.

**You'll need:**

A fireproof bowl or cauldron

1 pinch yarrow, for guidance and clarity

1 pinch sandalwood, for growth and grounding

1 pinch lemon balm, for healing and softness

1 pinch angelica, for introspection and emotional support

Shadow Work Journal and a prompt that you're stuck on

1 piece smoky quartz, for grounding and balance

1 piece amethyst, for introspection and self-awareness

A lighter

A charcoal disk

A pen

Place your fireproof bowl or cauldron in the middle of your workspace. Add each herb to the cauldron one by one, telling them their jobs by using the intentions in the ingredients list.

Place your journal flat in front of you with the cauldron behind it. On the left side of the cauldron, place your piece of smoky quartz. On the right, place your piece of amethyst.

Light your charcoal disk and stick it on top of the herbs. Once the herbs start smoking, run your pen through the smoke while saying: *Smoke and scent, move what is stuck. Clear my mind, and shift my luck. Let the truth beneath speak, soft but honest, slow and deep.*

Then begin writing. I know it might be hard to get your brain and spirit moving, so here are some clarifying prompts to help you out.

- "What is *actually* making this hard to write about?"
- "What do I *wish* I felt about this?"
- "What would I say to *someone else* who felt this?"
- "What would I say if *no one* could ever read this?"

Keep working on it for fifteen minutes. If after that time you still can't seem to write, try again tomorrow. Do not force yourself to sit there for hours. You'll just get frustrated and never want to do shadow work again.

# HERB BLEND BATCHES

**HERB BLENDS ARE SO FUCKING VERSATILE.** They have many uses and are super easy to prep. For this final part of the chapter, I'll give you the general method I use to make all my herb blends, plus three different recipes.

**You'll need:**

Your chosen herbs (choose a minimum of two; there is no max)

An essential oil that matches the intention (choose one to three intentions)

A mixing bowl

Disposable gloves

1 bay leaf

A nontoxic marker

A crystal that matches the intention (choose one intention)

Salt (optional)

A container or jar large enough to hold the mix

Add your herbs and essential oils to the bowl, telling each one why they're being tossed in there. Mix everything together with gloves because essential oils do not come off your hands easily.

On your bay leaf, draw a sigil with the marker that matches the intentions of your herbs. It can be a word or a phrase, but remember, it has to fit on a bay leaf. Place the bay leaf directly in the center of the bowl on top of the herb mixture.

Hold your crystal in your hands and whisper the affirmation listed in the recipe (page 114) to wake it up. Place it exactly on top of the bay leaf. Leave the bowl on your altar or under the moonlight or the sunlight to charge for four to eight hours. You can cut that time down to two to three hours by setting the bowl on top of some salt.

Once the time has elapsed, remove the crystal and crush the bay leaf into the herb blend. The bay leaf itself won't change the properties or alter the intentions for two reasons: One, the bay leaf has already been charged with the sigil and has adapted its intentions instead; two, bay leaves are well known for wish granting, and what is an intention if not a wish?

Mix the blend with your hands one more time and transfer it to your container. Place the crystal back on top of the herbs and close the lid. Usually, herb blends last for four to six months. If you see mold, throw it away. Repeat the chant whenever you use the blend.

**Ways to Use Herb Blends:**

- Add the blend to some hot water to use as a foot soak. Feet absorb energy faster, and it's like a mini spa day.
- Toss it all over your floors and sweep it from front to back. This releases the energy of the herbs into your space and helps you kick out the back door whatever negative vibes aren't supposed to be there.
- Throw some into a pot of boiling water for a fast simmer pot. The heat will release the vibes from the blends.

- Tuck a bit into your pillowcase. This charges you with the intentions while you sleep.
- Scatter some around the outside of your home for a bubble of whatever intention you choose.
- Add some to a bowl of hot water, drape a towel over your head, and let the steam seep into your pores.
- Press into wax seals to add energy and intention.
- Grind the herbs down to a powder and use a makeup brush to brush it all over your body (make sure the powders are all safe to breathe in because powder floats everywhere).
- Use as an offering to your spirit guides or the universe by leaving a small amount in a bowl on your altar.
- Stir a pinch into moon water (see page 16) for some DIY scrying (a form of divination where you stare into a reflective surface to find messages from your guides). Stare at the bowl and see if any messages appear through the herbs.
- Wrap herbs in a cloth, soak the cloth in warm water, and use it as a compress on your third eye, heart, or, literally, any part of your body.
- Sprinkle some in an envelope to send intentions to another person.

**NOTE: Before using any herb blend, make sure all ingredients are safe for inhalation and skin contact. Some herbs can cause allergic reactions, respiratory irritation, or skin sensitivity. Always research thoroughly and patch test when needed. When in doubt, consult a qualified herbalist or healthcare provider.**

## HEALING AND SELF LOVE BLEND RECIPE

**Intentions and Sigil Ideas:** Emotional healing, self-acceptance, forgiveness, inner peace, body positivity, mood support, grounding

| Herbs | Crystals | Essential Oils |
|---|---|---|
| Rose petals | Rose quartz | Sandalwood |
| Rose hips | Carnelian | Rose |
| Elderflower | Amethyst | Jasmine |
| Yarrow | Clear quartz | Cedar |
| Basil | Celestite | Lavender |

Chant: *By root and bloom, I call in care. Piece by piece, I repair. Breathe in calm, breath out pain. I call back joy to my name.*

## REBIRTH AND RENEWAL HERB BLEND RECIPE

**Intentions and Sigil Ideas:** Energetic reset, new cycles, inner rebirth, pattern breaking, accepting change, clean slate

| Herbs | Crystals | Essential Oils |
|---|---|---|
| Patchouli | Tiger's eye | Rosemary |
| Myrrh | Carnelian | Apple |
| Sandalwood | Selenite | Elderflower |
| Lemon balm | Bloodstone | Lilac |
| Rosemary | Clear quartz | Sandalwood |

Chant: *Fresh breath, clean slate. New path, new fate. I release what holds me to this place. I renew my soul and my space.*

## SPIRITUAL CONNECTION HERB BLEND RECIPE

**Intentions and Sigil Ideas:** Inner guidance, divine insight, soul clarity, shadow wisdom, higher knowing, ancestral links, intuition

| Herbs | Crystals | Essential Oils |
|---|---|---|
| Mugwort | Moonstone | Cinnamon |
| Frankincense | Labradorite | Chamomile |
| Jasmine | Fluorite | Yarrow |
| St. John's wort | Lapis lazuli | Myrrh |
| Damiana | Amethyst | Jasmine |

Chant: *Spirits speak, I'm here and still. I trust the message, I trust the will. I ask with clarity, not fear. If you're with me, this blend will make it clear.*

# 6

# SPRAYS, OILS + baths

Not everything in witchcraft has to be a dramatic-ass ritual. Sprays, oils, and baths are some of the laziest ways to work magic into your routine. You can bless a space in under five seconds, anoint your body with intention, or turn your daily shower into a self-care spell. Does setting them up take time? Absolutely. But once you have it done and ready to use, the flow of magic is easy.

Don't like baths? Same. Just toss your bath blends into a muslin, burlap, or cotton bag; tie it around your showerhead; and let the steam release the oils from the herbs. It's still magical, just minus the marination of the body in a tub of water.

A couple of things to remember for this chapter: One, if you're making a ritual spray and do not want to use rubbing alcohol, you need to use distilled water, witch hazel, or boiled water in its place. Alcohol preserves the sprays for longer than they would normally last by preventing mold and bacteria from forming. If you skip it, keep the spray in the fridge to help slow the molding process. Second, never put essential or fragrance oils directly onto skin. Aways dilute with a carrier oil for safety (see page 123 for more notes on carrier oils).

Now that that's out of the way, let's go spray some self-love.

# LOVE AND JOY SPRAY

**THIS SPRAY IS FOR DAYS WHEN YOU FEEL UNWORTHY,** to remind yourself that you don't need to prove yourself to be worth loving. Spray this when you forget you're allowed to take up space and like yourself.

**You'll need:**

Mug or heat-resistant bowl

1½-ounces (42 ml) boiled sun water or rose water

Rose petals, for harmony and healing

Jasmine, for anxiety relief and happiness

Basil, for peace and balance

Calendula, for blessings and pleasure

Strainer

2-ounce (60 ml) spray bottle

Gold, white, or pink paint marker, for glass

Rose or strawberry quartz chips, for compassion and comfort

½ ounce (14 ml) rubbing alcohol

Shimmer mica, for sparkles (optional)

Rose essential or fragrance oil (optional)

Fill your mug or bowl with the boiled sun water or rose water. Add the herbs in the following order, saying the following phrases out loud as you sprinkle each one in:

Rose petals: *Harmony and healing, come to me. Fill my soul with light and vibes of good company.*

Jasmine: *Anxiety calms. Happiness comes. Open my heart. Let stillness hum.*

Basil: *Balance my soul and bring peace to my aura. Let chaos leave and joy restore.*

Calendula: *Bless my space and bring pleasure to stay. Warm my spirit and brighten my day.*

Let the herbs steep in the water until the water is fully cooled. We want that shit to be potent as fuck. Once the water has cooled, strain out your herbs and place the "intention water" to the side. (Intention water is a completely made-up term that I use to describe water that isn't a tea but is still infused with herbs.)

On the spray bottle with your marker, write the words "love" and "joy." You can make them into a sigil if you want, but it's not necessary.

Add the crystal chips to the bottle and say: *Comfort and compassion in all that I do. Let me be kind to me, too.*

Add the alcohol to the spray bottle. Alcohol stops the water from molding as quickly as it normally would, so you need to make sure it has enough space in the bottle; that's why we're adding it first.

Next, add in your mica powder and essential oils, if you wish.

Last, top off the bottle with your intention water from earlier. Secure the cap, and that's it! Remember to shake it before each use.

Spray this all over your space after a hard journaling session to remind you to be kind to yourself. You can also use it on your pillow or bed when you feel a mental breakdown coming; it'll prep the space for crying as a release rather than crying from despair.

# CELEBRATING SUCCESSES SPRAY

**YOU DON'T NEED TO DO SOMETHING WILD** and huge to deserve a celebration. Doing shadow work even once is cause for celebration because many people wouldn't have even tried. We forget to celebrate our little successes, like finishing a video game we've been trying to beat or perfecting our winged eyeliner. This spray is for all the wins, big or small. This is your "fuck yeah, I did that—that was me" moment in a bottle.

**You'll need**

A small bowl

Sandalwood powder, for grounding and success

20 drops basil essential oil, for courage and confidence (see note)

20 drops rosemary essential oil, for pride and celebration (see note)

20 drops cedar essential oil, for growth and prosperity (see note)

A paintbrush

3 bay leaves

½ ounce (14 ml) rubbing alcohol

2-ounce (60 ml) spray bottle

Tiger's eye chips, for personal empowerment

Carnelian chips, for stepping into power

1 ounce (28 ml) distilled water

First, we need to make the "ink" for our sigils. Why are we doing this? Because markers bleed, and we don't want the chemicals seeping into our spray and flying around the house when we use it.

Grab your bowl, sandalwood powder, essential oils, and paintbrush.In the bowl, combine a few pinches of your sandalwood powder and ten drops of each essential oil. As you add them, tell each one what it's doing there. You can just repeat the intentions from the ingredients list to make your life easier. Use the paintbrush to mix the oils together in a clockwise motion to bring in that feeling of success. Say this while mixing:

*Blend this ink with will and fire; charge my sigil with true desire.*

Using your paintbrush and "ink," draw a sigil on each bay leaf. (Note that the "ink" does not actually have color, so it might be difficult to do any wildly intricate designs.) The first sigil should be for "empowerment." The second sigil should be for "celebration." And the last sigil should be for "success." You can follow the sigil tutorial on page 33. Set the bay leaves aside.

Now we can prepare the spray. Add your rubbing alcohol and remaining ten drops of each essential oil to the spray bottle. You can also pour in whatever liquid is left over from the sigil making. While you add them in, tell each one what they're doing, just like you did before. It's better to over intent than under.

Next, add your chips. Tell each one what they're doing there, just like you did for the oils.

Finally, add the bay leaves. Add them in the following order while chanting the corresponding affirmation. You can break them up to fit.

Empowerment: *My power is mine, abundant and true. I trust myself in all that I do.*

Celebration: *I don't need permission to celebrate me; I shine with joy, wild and free.*

Success: *I open doors and claim what's mine. My success and my soul always align.*

Fill the rest of the bottle with your distilled water, secure the cap, and shake as hard as you can.

Use this spray after completing a shadow work session to honor whatever the fuck you just processed. Or for a mini hype session before posting something vulnerable or stepping out of your comfort zone. Or to mark a turning point or completing a goal so you remember that any progress is still progress.

**NOTE: If you don't have essential oils, swap them for their dried versions and steep them in hot water. Strain out the plant matter and use the liquid as your base.**

# RELEASE MY ANGER OIL BLEND

**ANGER IS LIKE A CHAIN THAT DRAGS US SO FAR DOWN** that it seems impossible to get back on our feet. This oil blend will help us release all that anger, jealousy, self-hate, guilt, and resentment that might have come up during a session. The process is super easy and straightforward—I promise.

**You'll need:**

A few juniper berries, to control anger

A 10-milliliter glass roll-on bottle

Chamomile-scented oil, to soothe anger

Lavender-scented oil, to diffuse anger

Moonstone chips, for healing and release

1½ teaspoons (8 ml) carrier oil, such as avocado oil, sunflower oil, jojoba oil, or the ever-popular olive oil

Glass paint marker (see note)

Gather your ingredients, and let's do this shit. Start by adding a few juniper berries to your empty roll-on bottle. As you do so, say: *Control my anger.*

Next, add your chamomile oil. Say: *Soothe my anger.*

Add your lavender oil and say: *Diffuse my anger.*

Finally, add a few moonstone chips. Say: *I heal and release.*

Fill the rest of the bottle with your carrier oil. Cap the bottle, and shake it as hard as you can, almost as if you're trying to shake all those emotions out. Use your marker to write the word "soothe" on the outside of your bottle or make it into a sigil if you want to be a lil' extra.

Use this oil on your pressure points after shadow work or when you feel anger starting to make an appearance in your life. You can also use it to dress candles and for whatever else you can think of. But, mainly, it's an anointing oil.

**NOTE:** You can use permanent markers if you don't have or want to buy a paint marker. They're just super handy.

## A SHORT LESSON ON CARRIER OILS

There are a ton of carrier oils out there. Some are expensive as fuck; others accessible and common. Some have a nice light texture; others a deeper, heavier one. People tend to have a lot of feelings about this. Some hate that heavy, oily texture while others love it. Below is a list of possible carrier oils you can use in your witchcraft. You can use any of these in the oil blend spells in this chapter, depending on your preferences. If you can't match a certain intention, that's totally okay. You're not going to set intentions for the oils unless you want to.

| Oil Name | Price | Shelf Life | Texture | Intentions |
|---|---|---|---|---|
| Jojoba oil | $$$ | Up to 5 years | Light | Balance, stability |
| Fractionated coconut oil | $ | 1 to 2 years | Light | Purification, changes |
| Sweet almond oil | $$ | 1 year | Medium | Love, beauty |
| Sunflower oil | $ | 1 year | Medium | Joy, positivity |
| Olive oil | $ | 1 to 2 years | Heavy | Power, energy |
| Grapeseed oil | $ | 6 to 12 months | Light | Manifestation, growth |
| Avocado oil | $$ | 1 year | Heavy | Grounding, beauty |
| Rose hip oil | $$$ | 6 to 12 months | Light | Healing, grief |

**PRO TIP:** Charge your oil overnight in the moonlight to make the oil version of moon water.

Sacred
Rebirth
Room Mist

# SACRED REBIRTH ROOM MIST

**OKAY, SO YOU DID YOUR SHADOW WORK.** Now WHAT THE FUCK are we supposed to do with that pain? Those emotions we just brought to the table and left to converse amongst themselves need to be addressed. So, we're going to take that pain and turn it into power, energy, and the will to live.

**You'll need:**

4-ounce (120 ml) spray bottle

Myrrh, for rebirth

Sandalwood, for rebirth

Copal, for transmutation

Frankincense, for transformation

3 ounces (90 ml) moon water (see page 16)

½ ounce (14 ml) rubbing alcohol or witch hazel

Strainer

Essential or fragrance oil of your choice (optional)

Amethyst chips, for transmutation

Moss agate chips, for transformation

I designed this spell to not dirty too many items, so we'll build and make it in the same bottle.

Grab your spray bottle and begin adding in your herbs and resins (myrrh, sandalwood, copal, and frankincense). As you adding them in, repeat this chant for each one: *Take my pain, make it power. Transmute my fears, make them fire.*

Fill your bottle with the moon water and rubbing alcohol or witch hazel. Cap it and stick it in your fridge overnight, or for at least three hours at the minimum.

Once everything has had a chance to blend and steep, strain it out. Toss the spell remnants in the trash, and pour the strained water back into your spray bottle. At this stage, you can add any essential oils you want or that you just like to smell because we're spraying this all over the house.

Add your crystal chips to fill the rest of the bottle. Cap it and shake it as hard as you can.

Mist each corner of each room in your house. Every time you spray, say the following: *With this mist that fills my home, a sacred blend will keep me whole. Take my distress, take my pain; make it into only gains. With this mist that fills my home, I own my pain and the power it holds.*

Repeat the spraying process once every couple of weeks to remind your pain that it's actually power in disguise.

# FIRE IN THE SOUL OIL BLEND

**THIS OIL FOCUSES ON REBIRTH AND RENEWAL** by reigniting your passion for living. It was made to revive your inner fire when life feels dull, repetitive, or disconnected. When you've been numb for too long, this is your reminder that you were meant to burn as bright as you can.

**You'll need:**
A jar (see note)

2 to 5 of the following herbs in equal parts:

- Calendula, for solar energy and pleasure
- Lemon balm, to awaken your soul
- Patchouli, for luck and rebirth
- Rosemary, for warmth and vitality
- Galangal root, for enchantment and stimulation

1 piece carnelian, for manifestation and energy

1 piece clear quartz, for amplification

Olive oil or carrier oil of your choice (see note)

Patience or a forgetful memory

Place your jar in the middle of your workspace and add all of your herbs in equal parts. The herbs should fill up 90 percent of the space in your jar. While you add them, set your intentions using the ingredients list. For example: *Patchouli, you're here to bring me good luck and rebirth.* Super simple.

Next, add your crystals. Place them inside the jar, right on top of the herbs.

Fill your jar with oil. There will be hella air bubbles, so fill it, let it sit, and then fill it some more. Keep doing that until the jar is completely full of oil.

Secure the lid and shake as hard as you can. (Okay, not too hard, though, because you don't want to break the jar with the crystals—think soft chaos.) This shake will activate the ingredients, blend them together, and seal the intention. While you're shaking the jar, say: *Fire inside, ignite and roam free. Let this oil return power to me. The flames in my soul that have gone out, I breathe in new life and release my doubts. Confidence shine and awaken my soul. With this oil, I reclaim control.*

Place the oil in a cool, dark place (the back of a cabinet is best) and leave it there for one to three weeks (thus, the forgetful memory in the ingredients list). This lets the herbs and oil really blend together and create that potent fire oil we want.

After the time has passed, use the oil directly from the jar or transfer it to a smaller bottle. There's no need to strain, but if you do, discard the herbs like you normally would.

Use this oil after shadow work to reawaken the reasons why you're still here. Anoint your chest or wrists when you feel dull, stuck, or numb.

**NOTE:** The amount of oil you'll need for this spell depends on the size jar you have.

# DROP THAT SHIT BATH BLEND

**IN THIS SPELL,** we'll get rid of emotional residue, old identities, and bullshit that we're just so ready to get the fuck over so we can focus on rebirth, spiritual cleansing, and energetic resets.

**You'll need:**

2 pieces of paper and a pen

A small mixing bowl

½ cup (150 g) sea salt

1 teaspoon (3 g) patchouli, for release and desire

1 teaspoon (7 g) yarrow, for change and healing

1 teaspoon (1 g) basil, for power and trust

2 tablespoons (28 ml) your preferred carrier oil (see page 123)

6 drops juniper essential oil, for transformation and new beginnings

6 drops cedar essential oil, for balance and introspection

1 piece lapis lazuli, to release

1 piece clear quartz, to attract

On one piece of paper, write down everything you want to let go of. On the second piece, write everything you want to bring in to replace that energy. Put those to the side.

In your mixing bowl, combine your salt, herbs, carrier oil, and essential oils. Use the ingredients list to set intentions.

Once everything is combined, begin charging the mix. Place your bowl in the center of your workspace. On the left, place the paper with everything you want to release. On the right, place the paper with everything you want to bring in.

Hold the lapis lazuli and say: *I release the weight that is not mine.*

Place the crystal on the left side of your bowl on top of the release paper. Next, hold the clear quartz in your hands and say: *I call in what's aligned, what's true and what's mine.*

Place the crystal on the right side of the bowl on top of the "bringing in" paper. Wave both hands over the entire setup and say: *What I release is gone, bringing in a new dawn. What I call in is coming, bringing a vibrant humming. I drop that shit and let it go. I make space for the new and banish the old.*

Imagine your energy flowing out of your left hand, pushing things away. The energy in your right hand is pulling things in.

Discard the "release" paper outside of your home and place the "bringing in" paper on your altar. To use this in a bath, fill up your tub with warm water and pour in your bath blend. Soak for a minimum of five minutes or as long as you want. Use immediately or store it in an airtight container for up to a month.

Use this bath blend after a heavy shadow work session before starting a new thing, after doing a deep clean, or when you finally say to yourself, "I can't keep doing this shit."

# CALM THE ACTUAL FUCK DOWN, BESTIE OIL BLEND

**THIS IS YOUR OIL FOR WHEN YOU NEED TO FUCKING BREATHE.** It's an "exhale the bullshit and inhale the good shit" type of spell. When you're spiraling, when everything feels like it's going downhill, this oil blend will bring your peace back by calming your anxiety and letting your body know that it is not, in fact, in danger.

**You'll need:**

A piece of paper and pen

A 10-milliliter glass roll-on bottle

Lighter or matches

Pink candle

Rose petals, for healing and compassion

Chamomile flowers, for harmony and inner peace

Lavender or elderflower, for anxiety and working through emotions

Yarrow or St. John's wort, for purification and inner strength

1 piece rose quartz, for comfort and compassion

1 piece amethyst, for transmutation and anxiety relief

6 drops rose essential oil, to reinforce healing

1½ teaspoons (8 ml) rose hip oil or carrier oil of your choice

Set the mood for this spell by spraying your favorite perfume or putting on your comfort music. Anything that'll make you feel relaxation in your soul. Next, get your pen and paper and write a motivational, encouraging, self-love letter to yourself. You can pretend you're talking about your best friend if that helps. For example:

"Hey. I just want to remind you how hard you're trying. You've survived every hard thing that's been thrown your way so far. You show up with your full heart, even when you have nothing left to give. You're not perfect, but you're perfect for me. You're unstoppable, and you've got this."

Once you're done, fold the paper twice toward you. Place the love letter in the middle of your workspace. Place your dropper bottle on top of the paper.

Light the pink candle and let the wax bind the dropper bottle to the paper by dripping it around the bottom edge of the bottle. Blow out your candle and put it to the side.

Add a pinch of each of your herbs to your bottle one at a time. While you do this, think of how much you've overcome. Think about all of the things you thought were the end of the world but were just super fucking hard. Think about how you have shown up for yourself every day of your entire life no matter how hard you thought it was going to be. I'm not saying you should have had to. You shouldn't have had to be strong. I'm saying you did it anyway and survived.

Once everything is in there, place your rose quartz and amethyst on each side of the dropper bottle. Then add six drops of rose essential oil. (You can do more than this, but six is the number for inner healing and comfort, so try to keep it in multiples of six.)

Fill the rest of your jar with rose hip oil or whatever carrier oil you chose. Secure the cap and take a deep breath. Count to four as an inhale, then four counts to hold it in, and four counts to release it. Do this as many times as you need.

After you've remembered that you need to breathe to stay alive, go ahead and recite the following chant while holding onto the bottle: *Calm my mind, and ease my soul. Bring my emotions back to make me whole. I am loved, and I am safe. With this oil, I remember I am brave. Let peace return and fear release. My heart is steady, my breath at ease.*

Leave the oil in the exact same position overnight. In the morning, gently remove the bottle from the paper and place the letter somewhere on your altar. When your oil is not in use, place it on the letter to continuously charge the oil just like you would with a crystal plate.

Use on pulse points before sleep or hard conversations. Keep the roller in your bag or pocket for public anxiety attacks or panic.

Bless That Shit Spray

# BLESS THAT SHIT SPRAY

**OUR TOOLS ABSORB ENERGY** just like anything else we use for witchcraft, which means we need to clean and bless that shit. This spray instantly purifies and says, "Hey, you're sacred now," while adding some extra clarity and spiritual connection to make it easier for your guides to assist you in future spells. When your tools need cleansing and your energy needs balancing after a tough session or two, use this spray.

**You'll need:**

Empty tea bag

Peppermint, for clarity and focus

Yarrow, for balance and blessings

Mugwort, for spiritual connection and intuition

1½ ounces (42 ml) rainwater in a cup

½ ounce (14 ml) rubbing alcohol

2 ounce (60 ml) spray bottle

Sea salt, for purification and grounding

Blue lace agate chips, for divine wisdom and connections (see note)

Selenite plate, for blessing and cleansing (see note)

Start by filling your empty tea bag with your herbs (NOT THE SALT). We're setting intentions at the end so there's no need to do that now unless you want to. Place the filled tea bag in the rainwater and stick it in the fridge. Leave it in there for three hours.

Add the rubbing alcohol to the spray bottle. Add in a few pinches of sea salt and your blue lace agate chips. Secure the cap and shake the shit out of the bottle until your salt is fully dissolved.

Unscrew the cap and fill the rest of your bottle with the intention water you have in the fridge. Toss the used tea bag in the trash. You can also save the herbs inside, dry them out, and use them as an incense if you wish.

Close the bottle and hold it in your hands. Say the following chant three times: *Balance me and bless this space. Let spirit speak and communicate with grace.*

Place the bottle on top of your selenite plate overnight. If you don't have one, place it outside under the moonlight. After it's charged, it's ready to use.

Spray it on tarot cards, pendulums, or divination tools to help communication with spirit. Bless new tools or spray on your hands to call in clean energy and clarity.

**NOTE: You can use any shape of selenite plate as long as your bottle fits on top of it. Note that selenite is not water-safe; it disintegrates in water and becomes toxic, so be careful to keep the plate dry at all times. Substitute clear quartz chips for blue lace agate if you don't have it.**

# CAUTION: FLOWERS UNDER CONSTRUCTION BATH RITUAL

**WE'RE NOT ERASING THE PAIN WITH THIS BATH,** we're holding space for it. Basically, we're using flowers to mend our souls.

**You will need:**

½ cup (150 g) pink salt

¼ cup (28 g) dried calendula, for guidance

¼ cup (32 g) dried rose petals, for self-love

A fresh bouquet of wildflowers (see note)

10 drops rose essential oil (see note)

5 drops lavender essential oil

5 drops jasmine essential oil

Your favorite floral liquid soap, for bubbles (optional)

**NOTE: You can use any flowers for this bath as long as you're not allergic to them. Just make sure you know exactly what the flowers are when you pick them. Like, check them against a book or the internet—you do NOT want to end up soaking in a tub of poison oak because you didn't know what it looked like. You can switch the oils in this spell for any floral oil of your choice.**

Fill your tub and grab your favorite book and a glass of wine if you wish. When your tub is filled, add your ingredients one by one.

Add the pink salt first, and say: *Salt of earth, fill me with grace. Cleanse my body, soul, and space.*

Next, add your calendula and say: *Bloom through sorrow, bring me light. Guide my heart from pain to right.*

Next, add your rose petals. Say: *Love me soft, and love me deep. Comfort what I could not keep.*

You can either take the stems off the wildflowers and put them in the bathwater or you can keep them whole and place them around the edges of your bathtub. Either way, as you add them, say: *Grown in chaos, wild and true, may I bloom like you do.*

Finally, add the essential oils to the bath. As you do, repeat the following chant three times: *From root to heart this blend restores, from my body to my core. Calm my mind and bless my skin, with every drop, I mend within.*

If you're adding bubbles, this is the time to pour them in.

Once you're ready, slowly step into the tub. As you enter, say: *I enter this water with every part of me.*

Soak for as long as you want. Relax. Breathe deep. Let the flowers mend your soul.

Use this when you need grief support or healing from heartbreak or betrayal. Use it when you need to repair the trust inside of yourself or when you're spiraling in self-blame or guilt.

# STOP THAT SHIT OIL BLEND

**WE ALL HAVE ADDICTIONS.** And, no, I'm not talking about your vape or marijuana stash. I'm talking about that bad habit of overexplaining because your shadow is scared to be outcasted. Or when your manifestations are stuck because you keep running back to the same person, place, or thing that you were supposed to release. When your patience always runs thin and you have that little anger outburst that you've been trying to stop. Change takes a lot of work to go along with your magic. This oil won't save you from yourself, but it will support the part of you that's done with your own bullshit.

**You'll need:**

A small pot and spoon

3½ ounces (100 ml) coconut oil or carrier oil of your choice

Lemon balm, for cutting energetic ties

Agrimony, for breaking habits

Rosemary, for self-control

Chamomile, to calm emotions and soothe panic

Angelica, to break negative attachments

An empty tea bag

4-ounce (120 ml) dropper bottle

25 drops rosemary essential oil, to awaken senses

Fluorite chips, for self-discipline and growth

Place your pot on the stove and add in your coconut oil. We don't want it to boil, but we do want it to be hot, so leave it on medium heat for six minutes.

While the oil is heating, add your herbs to the tea bag, and then add the bag to your heated oil.

After the six minutes are up, reduce the heat to its lowest setting and let the herbs steep for around ten minutes. Afterward, turn the heat off and let it cool fully.

Once cooled, remove the tea bag and toss it in the trash.

Next, grab your dropper bottle and add the rosemary essential oil. The number for change, growth, and overcoming addictions is five, so we add twenty-five drops to keep it in multiples of five.

Next, add your fluorite chips to the dropper bottle, and then finish by adding the cooled seasoned oil. Replace the cap and shake it. While you shake, say: *Rosemary wakes my sleepy mind. Chamomile keeps my soul aligned. Agrimony breaks the pattern; lemon balm clears the clatter. Angelica makes the bullshit clear; rosemary lets self-control appear. Fluorite grounds me in my path, disciplined, focused, and free from wrath.*

I suggest writing the chant somewhere you can access it easily, like on your phone's notes app. That way, when you do use this oil, you can repeat the chant each time to remind you of the intent. Use daily to support change and reaching your goals. Anoint your third eye for focus and control.

# SOAK & SEE BATH RITUAL

**IN THIS MINI RITUAL,** we'll infuse our bath with a powerful bath blend to encourage deep visualization, clarity, and spiritual connection. This spell will give clarity when a shadow work session has left you more confused than when you started. It also helps strengthen your manifestations and goals by helping you imagine the life you want to create. We will make enough oil blend for four rituals. Please note that this spell is best done during a full moon to strengthen its potential. Is it required? No. Is it sternly suggested? Yes.

**You'll need:**

8 bay leaves, for wish fulfillment and strengthening spells

A nontoxic marker

½ cup (150 g) black salt (see note)

1 cup (300 g) sea salt

Large mixing bowl

Disposable gloves

4 tablespoons (45 ml) carrier oil of your choice

10 drops sandalwood essential oil, for deepening the ritual state

8 drops rose essential oil, for reconnection and self-worth

4 tablespoons (8 g) mugwort, for spiritual connection and intuition

4 tablespoons (2 g) peppermint, for psychic clarity and wisdom

5 drops cinnamon essential oil, for action and speed

A 16-ounce (470 ml) jar

**The Blend**

Start by cleansing your space, both physically and spiritually.

On your bay leaves with the marker, draw sigils for the following intentions: intuition, connection, reconnection, self-worth, spirit guides, manifestation, clarity, and awakening. Set them aside.

Add the salts to a large mixing bowl and use gloves to mix them together with your hands.

Next, add in your carrier oil of choice. Mix that in as well.

Add the essential oils one at a time while saying the following chant: *Fire to move, wood to hold. Bloom to soften what's frozen cold. With these oils, I rise in power. Steady and clear. This is my hour.*

Mix the contents of the bowl to blend again.

Next, add your herbs in any order your heart desires. Tell each one what they're doing there by repeating the intentions in the ingredients list. Add the bay leaves last, crushing them one by one. Mix everything together with your hands one last time. Transfer the blend to your jar, secure the lid, and you're done.

**You'll need:**

Paper and Pen

Tape (optional)

Moonstone, amethyst, lapis lazuli, and/or fluorite (optional)

**The Ritual**

Write the goals you wish to achieve on the sheet of paper and place it somewhere you'll be able to see throughout the entire ritual. I suggest taping it to the wall.

Dress the perimeter of the tub with the crystals you chose. While you place each one down, tell it why it's here using the ingredients list. For example, *rose essential oil, bring me reconnection and self-worth*. Place them in whatever order you want and wherever they fit. If your tub doesn't have a ledge, you can place them on the floor. Then, fill the tub and scatter about one-fourth of your bath blend over the water.

Step into the tub and soak in silence for two to five minutes. Then, start your visualization. Imagine what it will feel like when your goals are met. Visualize details, moments, sounds, smells—anything that you think will happen as well as anything you want to happen. Be as specific and as detailed as possible.

When you're ready to get out, say: *It is seen, it is known, it is mine.*

Use this when you feel disconnected from your goals, hopes, and dreams or after journaling to seal in desires.

**NOTE:** **Black salt will potentially stain your tub, so sub in sea salt if you're not feeling the whole cleaning part when you're done.**

# 7

# candles + CONTAINER SPELLS

Candle spells and container spells are my two favorite ways to do spell work because there are so many possibilities.

When it comes to candle spells, the first thing to think about is safety. When dressing your tealight, jar, and votive candles, keep the herbs and oils away from the wick. Tossing herbs onto the wick causes the herbs to catch fire and turns into a giant hazard. For chime and taper candles, a fire is inevitable, especially if we're using oils. I suggest lighting your candles in cauldrons or on fireproof plates. This contains the fire better than when it's in a normal candleholder. Keep a jar of sand or salt nearby at all times to dump on candles that get a little too spicy. Pro tip: If you can afford a candle lamp, get one. The lamp melts the wax, releasing the aromas and magic, and keeps the candle going for longer since there's no fire involved; as a bonus, you don't need to be on high alert at all times.

Candle magic and color magic are the best combos. Match your candle's intention to the color of the candle to raise the potency of your spell. Oh, and don't fucking listen to the people who say you can't blow out your candle because it's bad luck. Those people don't remember the point of birthday candles. (That being said, if you have loose herbs chilling on top of the candle, they'll fly all over the place.)

Container spells are even simpler, which is why we all love them. All you do is set intentions, toss your ingredients in, and seal the container. Done.

The flexibility and ease of these types of spells make them excellent options for adding magic to our shadow work journeys with as little extra work as possible.

# EVENING ESSENCE RENEWAL CANDLE RITUAL

**WE'RE NOT TRYING TO FIX** everything tonight, and we're not chasing peace either. We're just trying to breathe and give ourselves space to feel like a whole fucking person again after some intense shadow work. This ritual is your exhale; it helps you quiet the noise and come back to yourself. You're allowed to rest, and this is your reminder to do so.

**You'll need:**
Eucalyptus jar candle or other calming scent

Lighter or matches

Rosemary, for release and renewal

Patchouli, for spiritual grounding and stillness

Amethyst, for energetic reset

Selenite, for cleansing and calm

Small dish of moon water (see page 16)

Place your candle in the middle of your workspace. Light it, and let the top layer melt completely.

Once it's melted, blow out the flame and add your herbs. Please remember to keep the herbs away from the wick so they don't catch fire when you relight the candle.

When adding herbs, follow these chants. First, add your rosemary. Say: *I release the day. I reclaim my peace.*

Next, add your patchouli and say: "*I am connected and safe. My mind stays grounded.*"

Place your amethyst and selenite on each side of your candle. Make sure they're touching the actual jar. Place your small bowl of water in front of the jar and crystals.

Relight your candle, take a few deep breaths, and say: *I light this flame to clear my space.*

Gaze into the flame and visualize it melting away anything that's clinging to you (stress, guilt, anger, jealousy). Do this for a few moments. When you're ready, dip your dominant hand's pointer finger in the water. Drip some water on your third eye first. Say: *No more noise, no more fear; my thoughts grow calm and clear.*

Next, dab a bit on your heart (it's on the left side of your chest in case your forgot) and say: *What I carry I now release, put in its place a bit of peace.*

Last, put a bit on your wrists. Say: *I rest without worry and sleep without fear, I create a space for time to heal.*

Gaze into the candle once more before closing your eyes and saying: *My work is done, the peace is here. I rest in calm, my rest is near.*

Blow out your candle, say thank you, and go the fuck to sleep—or watch your favorite movie.

Use this candle to clear away any bullshit that's left on your aura from the day, to ground yourself before you go to sleep, or simply to reconnect to your peace, purpose, and higher self.

# MAKE-AHEAD AFFIRMATION CANDLES

**THESE CANDLES ARE FOR THE DAYS** when you forget who the fuck you are and just need a gentle reminder. They're confidence on standby. They're candles that hold strength for you. Unlike the other spells in this chapter, these candles carry the memory of your magic, so you can make them ahead of time. So, when you need them—like after a tough shadow work session, for example—all you'll need to activate the candles is a lighter.

**You'll need:**

Toothpick or candle-carving tool

4 white, red, orange, yellow, or brown chime candles

A steel, silicone, or ceramic tray long enough to lay your candles down in

Basil, for success and joy

Nettle, for confidence and strength

Mullein leaf, for courage and purpose

Hibiscus powder, for love and attraction

3-4 milliliters olive oil, for empowerment and manifestation

10 drops rosemary essential oil, for clarity and focus

Small mixing bowl

A paintbrush (optional)

Container to hold the finished candles

We'll start by carving our candles. Using your toothpick, carve the words "empowerment" and "confidence" into all four candles. You can also make these words into a sigil and carve that instead. Set your candles aside.

Place your tray in the middle of your workspace. Sprinkle the herbs onto the tray, one by one, while chanting these affirmations (the order doesn't matter):

Basil: *I am meant to thrive. Joy belongs to me.*

Nettle: *I am stronger than I remember. I speak with power.*

Mullein leaf: *I show up, even when I'm scared. I move through fear with grace.*

Hibiscus: *I attract what aligns with me. I am magnetic.*

Next, mix together your olive oil and rosemary essential oil in your small mixing bowl. As you mix them, say: *I blend empowerment and clarity. Each drop holds infinite power.*

Dip your paintbrush into the oil mixture and brush it all over your candles. You can use your fingers, but oil is so annoying to get off; you'll smell like rosemary until you take a full shower.

Roll one of your oiled-up candles in the tray of herbs. The herbs should stick to the candle on their own. It doesn't need to be perfect; it just needs to be on there for the most part. Do this with all four candles. You can sprinkle in some more herbs as you go; just remember to repeat the affirmations again if you do.

Place your finished candles in a container of your choice. I suggest a box lined with parchment paper.

When you want to light one of the candles, repeat this affirmation: *I remember who I am. I love who I am. I burn brighter every time.*

I suggest writing the affirmation down on a small piece of paper and keeping it inside the container with the candles so you don't have to find this page in the book every time.

Use these affirmation candles when your confidence is low, when you need a reminder of how badass you are, or if you're mid-spiral with no energy to do a whole-ass spell.

**NOTE:** Whether you bought jars, envelopes, spell bags, etc. in bulk or just did a fire haul from the metaphysical shop, leave the whole haul/case of "equipment" outside under the moonlight. This will cleanse it for you and you won't have to remember to do it for each spell. Same with ingredients like herbs and crystals.

# EMOTIONAL FREEZE

**WHEN WE DO SHADOW WORK,** we're literally pulling our guilt and shame to the front. Personally, once I'm done analyzing my shadow self, I have a hard time letting go of that energy so I can continue my day/week/month/life without dwelling on the "Oh shit, I'm a horrible person—let me just jump into traffic." Ya know? So, I created this spell to help let that shit go. In theory, we will "freeze" those emotions until the next time we do shadow work while at the same time using these herbs and crystals to soothe said emotions while they're "out of commission."

**You'll need:**
A white envelope (eco-friendly preferred)

Paper

Pencil

Basil, for courage and clarity

Mullein leaf, for balance and grounding

Lavender, for release and healing

Moss agate chips, for growth, transformation, and grounding

Lighter or matches

White, purple, or blue candle, for sealing and activating

Freezer

First, get your shit together. If you have the time, energy, and patience, cleanse your envelope with some incense smoke. If not, fuck it; the universe knew what you meant anyway (see note).

Now, on your paper, write down the shadow qualities you've unearthed from your current shadow work sessions. Write it down, even if you only found out one thing about yourself. Fold the paper AWAY from you since you want those feelings to stay away from you until a later date and time. Stick your folded paper into the envelope. Add the basil, mullein leaf, lavender, and moss agate chips to the envelope.

To activate the spell, light your candle and seal the envelope with candle wax. Make sure you cover the entire opening with wax. While you're doing this (it'll take two to four minutes to get it all sealed), chant the following, repeating as long as it takes you to finish sealing the envelope:

*Basil, mullein, lavender, moss. Take these feelings and hide them but do not make them lost. These feelings are a part of me, I know this to be true. I put them in the freezer to pause, not to undo. Let them wait and rest with ease, never leaving me empty. I set them free until I am ready.*

Once you're done sealing, put the envelope in the freezer. (Maybe warn everyone in your household not to fucking touch it or, alternatively, put it in a bag that says "NO TOUCHY" or something like that.) Leave it in the freezer until it's time to come back to your shadow work. When it's time, take the envelope out of the freezer and keep it by you while you answer your shadow work questions. Put it back when you're done, and take the envelope out each time you do a particularly emotional shadow work session. You don't need to redo your envelope unless you feel you need to. At a minimum, try to remake it every six to eight months.

# THE BALANCING ACT CANDLE RITUAL

**OUR ENTIRE LIVES ARE BALANCING ACTS.** We are always tipping the scales, one way or another. But you don't have to choose between rest and action. This ritual holds space for both. It's about moving with purpose, not just moving to survive.

**You'll need:**

- Black chime candle
- A knife or scissors
- Candle-carving tool or toothpick
- Frankincense oil, for balance
- Cinnamon powder, for action
- Lighter
- Fire-safe bowl or cauldron
- White tealight
- Chamomile powder, for patience

Start by dressing your candles. Cut the black chime candle in half with your knife or scissors. Yes, I'm serious; just do it. We want the chime and tealight to burn at the same speed. Chime candles take forever, and we don't have time for all of that. Take your carving tool and write the word "action" on the top half of the chime candle—the half with the wick. Save the bottom half for future spell jars that require a wax seal.

Rub a little frankincense oil over the candle, then sprinkle cinnamon powder on top of the oil. Melt the bottom of the candle with a lighter, and stick it in your cauldron or fireproof bowl. Then, place the whole thing in the middle of your workspace.

Carve the word "patience" into your tealight. If it doesn't fit, make a sigil for it instead. Add a few drops of your frankincense oil around the tealight, and sprinkle the chamomile powder on top of that. Make sure to keep both ingredients away from the wick. Place the dressed tealight in front of the bowl with the chime candle.

Light your tealight first. Say: *Stillness brings wisdom, I am patient.*

Take seven deep breaths. Then, light your chime candle and say: *Now I move with care and fire.*

Take another seven deep breaths and say: *I move when it's time, I wait when it's wise. I trust the stillness. I trust the highs. In balance, I wait for both to collide.*

Let the candles burn all the way down. When they're burned out, discard them in a trash can inside of the home.

Use this ritual when you're stuck overthinking and underdoing, when you have ideas and don't know where to start, or because you're burning out and you don't know how to rest. (I quite literally just called myself out for the sake of this book.)

# PEACE AND SERENITY SHAKER JAR

**THIS SPELL IS FOR PEOPLE** who don't know how to rest because they associate productivity with their self-worth. It's a reminder that you are allowed to want peace. We're not chasing calm on this spell; we're inviting it over for tea and cookies.

**You'll need:**

- Funnel
- A jar with a screw-top cap
- New moon or rainwater (see page 16)
- Moss agate or rose quartz chips
- Blue lace agate chips
- 3 bay leaves
- Lavender, for inner peace
- Chamomile, to calm and soothe anxiety
- Rose petals, for self-compassion and softness
- Elderflower, for harmony and healing
- Blue food coloring or mica powder (optional)
- A blue candle (optional)
- Lighter

First, fill the jar. Using either a funnel or pure grace, fill about half of the jar with half of your chosen water. As you do so, say: *I am calm.*

Next, we'll add in our chips. Start with your moss agate or rose quartz chips. Add them to the jar and say: *I am loved no matter what.* Say it two times. Then add the blue lace chips and say: *Peace lives within me.* Say it two times.

Hold your bay leaves in your hands and whisper: *Grant me the wish of peace and serenity. Let chaos fade and my soul move steadily.*

Add each leaf to your jar one by one. You can crush them if they don't fit but leave them whole if they can fit that way.

Next, add the herbs one by one, telling them their jobs as you do based on the intentions in the ingredients list. However, try to keep the intentions in first person. For example, lavender should sound something like: *I claim inner peace.* If you choose to use food coloring or mica powder, add that in now.

Fill the rest of the bottle with your chosen water, making sure to leave a little of the bottle empty so you have enough room to shake. Then secure the lid. If you have a blue candle, light it and use that now to seal the bottle. If not, the world isn't ending. The spell will still work.

To activate the spell jar, shake it as hard as you can. Do this every single time you need a hint of peace and serenity. Use this spell jar when you're feeling burned out, overstimulated, or under-loved, or while you're trying to rewire your brain to rest without guilt.

# CANDLE AND JOURNAL SESH

**YOU KNOW THAT FRIEND,** family member, or coworker you can call to tell them anything, and they always get you? This ritual is that kind of friend. It doesn't need explanations on why you're spiraling or shutting down. It just listens. In this spell, we will let the candle give us a safe space to vent with no filter. Sidenote: This spell will get messy.

**You'll need:**

Shadow Work Journal

Jar candle

Yarrow, for healing and release

Sandalwood, for clarity and inner wisdom (see note)

Lavender, for forgiveness and processing

Juniper berries, for self-trust and truth

Lighter or matches

Paintbrush or makeup brush

Pen or marker

Place your journal flat in front of you and your candle behind it.

Next, grab your herbs. Sprinkle them all over your journal and around the outside of the jar candle. Sprinkle them one by one and say the following affirmations for each as you do. Make this as messy as you want. This spell is made for you to be as messy as you can be with your emotions, and this act adds to that.

Yarrow: *I release my emotions.*

Sandalwood (or peppermint): *I process with wisdom.*

Lavender: *I forgive myself for holding back.*

Juniper berries: *I give myself the trust to speak my truth.*

Next, light your candle and say: *This flame is my truth reflected in ink.*

Use your paintbrush to brush the herbs off of your journal. Then open it and freewrite for ten to twenty minutes. Let the flame from the candle and the reassurance from the herbs rip the ugly feelings out. Don't try to sugarcoat it. Don't try to analyze it. Just feel it. Be authentic to you and you alone.

When you're done, close your journal and say: *I hold my truth with warmth and comfort. I release the shit that doesn't need to be in my life.*

Blow out your candle, and move on with your day.

Use this ritual when you're in a spiral, manic-induced or not. Use it when you've been holding on to too many things or when you feel alone with your emotions and no one around you understands.

**NOTE:** Sandalwood powder won't work for this one, so if you only have the powdered version, swap it out for peppermint.

# SWEET RELEASE ENVELOPE SPELL

**ENVELOPE SPELLS ARE PERFECT** for sealing your shadow work session. In this spell, we'll take what we've learned about ourselves (guilt, shame, resentment, anger, sadness, etc.) and release the disdain and hatred we feel for those findings. This is a two-part spell because there is a waiting period in between. Note that I did not list the intentions for each ingredient because they're all related to and associated with healing and release.

**You'll need:**

An envelope (bonus points if it's gold)

A pen

A list of your uncovered shadow traits from the latest journaling session

**At least four of the following herbs:**

- Elderflower
- Basil
- Lavender
- Rosemary
- St. John's wort
- Yarrow
- Mullein leaf

Candle wax

Juniper essential oil

1 piece celestite

**Part One**

Start by drawing a sigil for RELEASE on the front of the envelope (see page 33 to help guide you on how to make a sigil). If you don't feel like it, just write the actual word.

Place your list of shadow traits in front of you and sprinkle a bit of each herb onto the paper. Repeat the following chant a total of nine times while you're doing this to activate the herbs:

*With every herb, I send away the heavy weight of yesterday. Plants so light, carry me free. I breathe in hope, I let it be.*

Take a giant deep breath after the ninth time and start folding your paper. Fold it away from you to signify release while being careful to not let the herbs spill out. Once the list is small enough to fit in the envelope, place it inside. Seal the envelope either with candle wax or by licking the sticky part (I know, super technical language here). Place three drops of the juniper essential oil on the sealed part of the envelope.

Place the envelope on your altar and then place the piece of celestite on top. The celestite will cleanse, heal, and release that shit. Leave it on your altar overnight.

**You'll need:**
Matches or lighter

Cauldron or safe space to burn

Tweezers (optional)

**Part Two**

The following day, grab your envelope and head to your burning location. Light the envelope on fire, place it in your cauldron, and let it burn all the way down. It's cool if you have to light it multiple times; just make sure it's fully burned. I suggest you keep tweezers nearby in case the pieces get too small to hold and burn safely in your hand.

Once your envelope is fully burned, go outside and blow the ashes into the wind.

Thank the universe and cry if you have to. You're done!

# acknowledgments

I thought about dedicating this book to my shadow self, but she's already gotten enough attention. So instead, thank you to my little brother Alex—still the real MVP and the reason I didn't throw my laptop out the fucking window. To my partner, for loving me through the chaos. And to my therapist, thanks for not blocking my number.

# about the author

Born and raised in Tampa, Florida (with a detour in Atlanta, Georgia), **Andrea Samayoa** has been a practicing witch for seven years. She started Moon Street Kits, an Etsy shop and accompanying TikTok channel, in 2020 with the goal of making her space accessible to beginners and to end the stigma behind witchcraft. Her page has been a haven for beginners and generational witches alike who love her "no bullshit" approach that makes it easy for viewers to follow her tutorials and still feel like they're connecting with a real person with realistic goals.

# index

## F



## G



## H



## I



## L



## M



## N



## O



## P

## R



## S



## T



## Y



## Z